PRESCHOOL

The **IDEA MAGAZINE FOR TEACHERS**

MAILBOX

2013–2014 YEARBOOK

The Education Center, LLC
Greensboro, North Carolina

The Mailbox® 2013–2014 Preschool Yearbook

Managing Editor, *The Mailbox* Magazine: Kimberly A. Brugger

Editorial Team: Becky S. Andrews, Diane Badden, Kimberley Bruck, Karen A. Brudnak, Catherine Caudill, Pam Crane, Chris Curry, Brenda Fay, Tazmen Fisher Hansen, Marsha Heim, Lori Z. Henry, Troy Lawrence, Gary Phillips (COVER ARTIST), Mark Rainey, Greg D. Rieves, Rebecca Saunders, Sharon M. Tresino

ISBN 978-1-61276-527-3
ISSN 1088-5536

© 2014 The Education Center, LLC, PO Box 9753, Greensboro, NC 27429-0753

Printed in the United States of America.

The Mailbox® Yearbook
PO Box 6189
Harlan, IA 51593-1689

HPS256266

Contents

Departments

Features

Book Units

Center Units

Literacy Units

Math Units

Teacher Resource Units

Thematic Units

Index

ARTS & CRAFTS
FOR LITTLE HANDS

Arts & Crafts
for Little Hands

Process Art

Puzzle-Cut Prints

This idea develops visual discrimination skills! Press pot scrubbers in colorful paint and pat them on a large paper rectangle, overlapping the prints as you work. Puzzle-cut the dry artwork; then arrange and mount the resulting puzzle on a larger rectangle, leaving gaps between the pieces as shown.

Marlene Breihan
Notre Dame Preschool
St. Louis, MO

Love, Cicily

Hugs and Kisses

Here's a lovely gift that's just perfect for National Grandparents Day! Press a rubber stamp *X* and *O* in ink pads to make prints to decorate a tagboard frame. Mount a personal photo to an appropriately sized construction paper backing and attach the backing to the frame. Embellish this adorable keepsake with desired craft materials and attach a ribbon hanger.

inspired by an idea from Ada Goren
Winston-Salem, NC

Wave of Love

This simple poem reminds the handprint maker that waving means goodbye as well as hello! Press a colorfully painted hand on a sheet of construction paper to make a handprint. Then glue a copy of the poem from page 20 to the page. What a comforting reminder for someone missing her family that they will be reunited!

Jeannine Dupler
Gainesville, FL

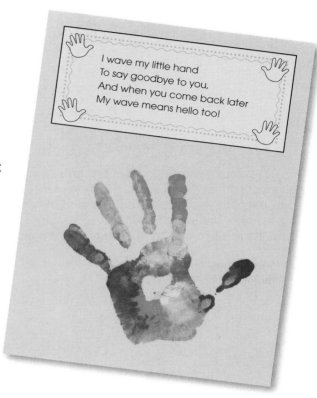

I wave my little hand
To say goodbye to you,
And when you come back later
My wave means hello too!

Process Art

Beneath the Burlap

Inexpensive burlap is the key to this unique project! Place burlap atop light-color construction paper and attach the layered materials to a clipboard. Paint the burlap thoroughly with desired colors of paint and then remove the burlap to reveal the artwork beneath!

Bridget Williamson
Bridget's Childcare
Sewell, NJ

Arts & Crafts
for Little Hands

Monster Mash

Dip a potato masher in paint and press it on a sheet of paper several times. (For artistic inspiration, play a recording of your favorite version of "Monster Mash" while you work!) Then use scrap paper and craft materials to transform each print into a monster.

Jennifer Gemar
Tripp-Delmont Elementary
Tripp, SD

Prize-Winning Pumpkin

Try this process-art idea to turn an ordinary pumpkin into eye-catching autumn decor! Spread diluted glue onto a pumpkin and press colorful tissue paper scraps on the glue, overlapping the tissue paper as desired. Spread a coat of glue on the tissue paper to create a decoupage effect; then sprinkle glitter on the glue. Beautiful!

Teri Lavelle
Zion Lutheran Preschool
Indiana, PA

Handsome Turkey

To make this turkey craft, paint the outside of a paper bowl brown and then glue it to a sheet of paper. Draw a turkey head, legs, and feet. Then glue craft feathers to the project so they resemble tail feathers. These 3-D turkeys turn out as unique as your little ones!

Christi Valenti
Miss Tara's Little Rascals
Massapequa, NY

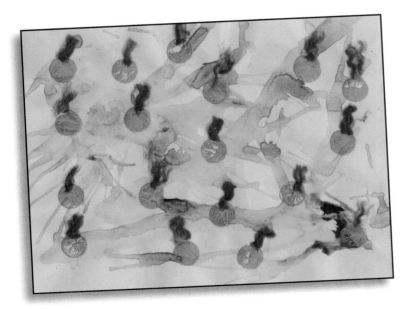

Pint-Size Pumpkins

The result of this process-art activity is a pumpkin patch full of mini pumpkins! Use a straw to blow thinned dark green paint (pumpkin vines) onto light green paper. Next, dip one end of a cork in orange paint and stamp it along the vines so the prints resemble pumpkins. Then glue a snippet of green or brown yarn (stem) to each pumpkin.

Mary Ann Craven
Fallbrook United Methodist Christian School
Fallbrook, CA

Web Designs

String-painting is fun, but pasta-painting is even more delightful! Dip a strand of cooked spaghetti in white paint and then drag it around on a web-shaped cutout. Repeat the process until the cutout resembles a spiderweb; then glue a plastic spider to the web.

Michelle Espelien
Crossroad Preschool
Minneapolis, MN

Lovely Autumn Leaf

Prepare several shallow containers of fall-colored paint and place a loose ball of crumpled aluminum foil near each container. Dip a ball of foil in paint and then press it on a manila leaf cutout. Repeat the process with other balls of foil and colors of paint until the cutout resembles a colorful fall leaf. Then glue pretzel sticks to the leaf to create veins and a stem.

Janet Boyce
Cokato, MN

Arts & Crafts
for Little Hands

A Snowy Pal

Youngsters are sure to enjoy making this adorable snowpal. To make a snowpal face, draw eyes and a mouth on a six-inch white paper circle and then glue an orange triangle (carrot nose) to it. Next, glue the snowpal to an eight-inch black circle. Glue the circles to a sheet of blue construction paper. Then decorate a pair of mitten cutouts as desired and glue them to the project as shown. To complete the project, dip the eraser of an unsharpened pencil in white paint and make prints (snowflakes) on the paper.

Janet Boyce
Cokato, MN

Kwanzaa Kinara

To make a kinara, glue a 2" x 7" brown paper rectangle near the bottom of a sheet of white construction paper. Dip a finger into a shallow container of black paint and then fingerpaint a candle above the center of the kinara. Also make a few black fingerprints around the edge of the paper. Dip a clean finger in red paint and then fingerpaint three candles to the left of the black one and add more fingerprints to the edge. Next, dip a clean finger in green paint. Fingerpaint three candles to the right of the black one and make several green fingerprints around the paper's edge. To complete the project, dip a clean finger in yellow paint and make a fingerprint flame above each candle.

Janet Boyce

Candy Cane Painting

Add more sensory fun to process art with mint-scented paint! Place red and green paint in containers and then mix peppermint extract in the paint. Hold a candy cane by the crook and dip the end in the paint. Then paint as desired on a sheet of paper. Finally, sprinkle glitter on the wet paint!

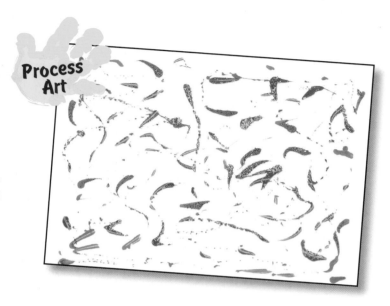

Process Art

Process Art

Dish Cleaner Fun!

To prepare, gather several dish cleaners with handles, such as those shown. Place each one next to a shallow container of paint. Then dip a cleaner in the corresponding paint and press, dab, tap, and swipe it on a sheet of paper to make a variety of marks. Continue with other cleaners.

adapted from an idea by Kathy Kelley
Bonsack Baptist Weekday Early Education Center
Roanoke, VA

Make this art seasonal!

Have little ones use the cleaners and white paint to make a snowstorm! Sprinkle salt on the wet paint to add some sparkle!

A Polar Show

To make the northern lights, rub colored chalk on a sheet of dark blue construction paper. Then glue a white semicircle (polar bear head) to the bottom of the paper. Draw eyes and a nose on the head and then glue two cotton balls (ears) beside the head. Next, stretch a cotton ball and glue it around the polar bear's eyes and nose. Finally, use a cotton swab to put dots of clear gel glue on the paper. Sprinkle glitter on the glue and then shake the paper over a tray to remove the excess glitter.

Janet Boyce
Cokato, MN

We Are Friends

Celebrate Dr. Martin Luther King Jr.'s birthday with this friendly craft. For each pair of young-sters, prepare two heart cutouts as shown. Turn the hearts upside down and have one child dip her right hand in flesh-colored paint and make a print on each heart. Then have the other child dip her left hand in flesh-colored paint and make a print that covers some of her partner's print on each heart. Encourage each child to write her name beneath her print. Finally, have her add a copy of the poem shown to her craft.

Barbara Sheridan
Humpty Dumpty Day Nursery
Greenlawn, NY

Mia   Sammie

Friends at school
Are tall and small.
Friends that care,
Friends that share—
We all need friends
Everywhere.

A Dental Masterpiece!

Celebrate National Children's Dental Health Month with this unique artwork! Use a toothbrush to add colorful paint to a sheet of paper. Use other toothbrushes and colors of paint as desired. Next, lay lengths of dental floss in the wet paint. (Add dots of glue to adhere the floss if needed.) Then cut a white paper strip into pieces (teeth). Glue the teeth to the paper.

Janet Boyce
Cokato, MN

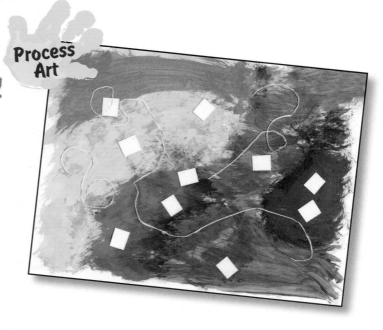

Process Art

Snazzy Snails

These adorable critters are perfect for a Valentine's Day display. To make a snail shell, squeeze white paint and red paint on a small paper plate. Then use a plastic spoon to mix and swirl the paint over the entire plate. Set it aside to dry. Next, trace your shoe, cut it out, and then decorate the cutout so it resembles a snail's body. Bend a length of sparkly pipe cleaner (antennae) and tape it to the back of the snail's body. Finally, glue the snail's shell to its body.

Janet Boyce

Wonderful Rainbows

What's at the end of a rainbow? A pot of gold, of course! Cut a portion of the rim from a paper plate. Paint the rim so it resembles a rainbow. When the paint is dry, glue a black pot to the end of the rainbow. Then glue crumpled yellow tissue paper squares (gold) at the top of the pot.

Paula Obringer
Kolbe's Korner
Westlake Village, CA

Process Art

Brushed Paintings

Youngsters are sure to enjoy creating these colorful masterpieces. Squirt several blobs of paint onto a sheet of construction paper. Turn the paper so that it is at an angle. Then use a clean hairbrush to brush the paint across the paper. After a desired effect has been reached, set the painting aside to dry.

Janet Boyce
Cokato, MN

Arts & Crafts
for Little Hands

Superbug

The result of this process art activity is a really big bug! To make a bug, fold a sheet of construction paper in half lengthwise. Unfold the paper and put dollops of paint along the fold line. Refold the paper and gently rub the surface; then unfold the paper and glue hole-reinforcer eyes, legs, and antennae to the print.

Janet Boyce
Cokato, MN

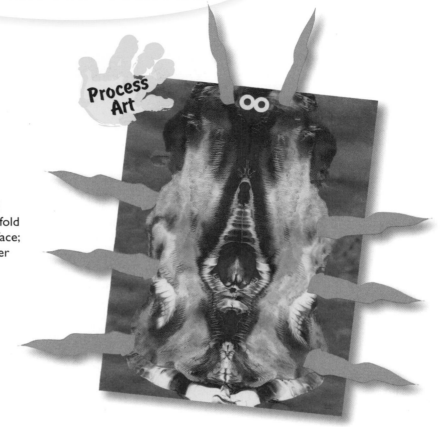

Process Art

Choir on a Wire

To make this picturesque scene, glue two brown rectangles (utility poles) and a length of black yarn (wire) to a sheet of blue construction paper as shown. Glue bird cutouts above the wire. To complete the scene, draw or stamp music notes around the birds so it looks like they are singing!

Garden Gate

Creating this cute springtime craft helps to develop fine-motor skills! Fold a 4½" x 12" paper rectangle card-style. Unfold the paper and cut a rectangle from one side as shown; then glue paper strips in place to create a gate. To make a flower garden, draw stems and leaves on the paper. Then make fingerprint flowers. When the paint is dry, close the gate as shown.

Janet Boyce, Cokato, MN

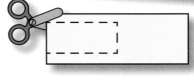

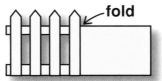

fold

Double-Sided Coaster

This heartwarming keepsake makes an adorable and practical Mother's Day gift! To make this double-sided coaster, make a handprint picture or a fingerprint design on a tagboard circle. When the paint is dry, laminate the circle and use tacky glue to attach it to a circle-shaped cork cutout. Then laminate a copy of the poem shown and glue it to the cork side of the coaster. How unique!

Meghan Mitchell
New Milford Early Learning Center
New Milford, NJ

I made this coaster for coffee or tea,
So when you relax you'll think of me.
The design was made with my own little hands.
You're the #1 Mom, and I'm your biggest fan!

Arts & Crafts
for Little Hands

"Tree-mendous" Fireworks!

Spotlight the Fourth of July with these fabulous fireworks! In advance, put red, white, and blue paint in separate shallow pans. Gather small pine tree twigs. Place the pans and twigs on a protected surface. To make this nighttime masterpiece, choose a branch, dip it in paint, and then slap it on a sheet of black construction paper. Repeat the process with other branches and colors of paint. Then sprinkle glitter on the wet paint. What lovely fireworks!

Susan Berry-Ruane
St. Stephen Preschool
Williamsburg, VA

Process Art

You are my sunshine.

A Sunny Day

Prepare shallow pans of orange and yellow paint. To make this sunny masterpiece, glue a yellow circle to a sheet of paper. Then roll a foam roller in a pan of paint and roll outward on the paper from the yellow circle. Continue, adding paint as needed, until the image looks like a sun with rays. Repeat the process with the other color of paint. Then use a craft stick to draw wiggly lines in the paint. When the paint is dry, decorate the sun with a photo and the caption shown.

Peanut Butter and Jellyfish

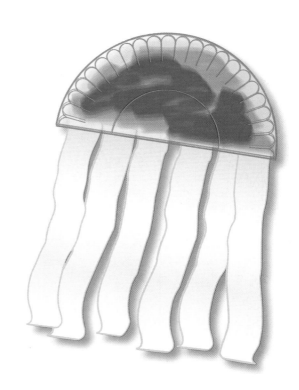

This whimsical little project looks terrific in an ocean-themed display! Get a clear plastic disposable plate (clear plates can be found in party supply stores and online) and cut it in half. Mix yellow and brown paint so it resembles the color of peanut butter. To begin, brush some of this mixture on the inside of one of the plate halves. Then brush purple paint (grape jelly) on the outside of the remaining half. Next, place the jelly plate half on the peanut butter half so the paint is sandwiched between the layers. Tape strips of plastic left over from laminating (or clear cellophane) to the back of the project. How cute!

Karen Cucinotta
Amherst Community Church Child Care Center
Amherst, NY

Process Art

Buddy Blending

This partner project is fun and easy! Fold a sheet of 12" x 18" construction paper in half lengthwise. Trim plastic cards (like the kind found in junk mail offers) to make paint scrapers. Then gather two youngsters. Have one child choose a primary paint color. Then have him use a foam roller to roll the paint on one half of the paper. Have a second child repeat the process with a different primary paint color and the remaining half of the paper. Then refold the paper and have students smooth it with their hands. Unfold the paper and look at the result. Finally, have each child add lines to his side of the paper with paint scrapers.

adapted from an idea by Janet Boyce
Hinojosa Early Childhood and Pre-Kindergarten Center
Houston, TX

Poem Cards

Use with "Wave of Love" on page 7.

I wave my little hand
To say goodbye to you,
And when you come back later
My wave means hello too!

TEC41068

I wave my little hand
To say goodbye to you,
And when you come back later
My wave means hello too!

TEC41068

I wave my little hand
To say goodbye to you,
And when you come back later
My wave means hello too!

TEC41068

CIRCLE TIME

Circle Time

Search and Sit

Youngsters get acquainted with this fun version of hide-and-seek! Print a large photo of each child; then scatter the photos facedown around the classroom. To play, hide your eyes and count to ten, making sure to count loud and slow. As you count, each child finds one photo and quickly sits in your circle-time area before you reach ten. When all the students have returned and you finish counting, give them a round of applause for returning so quickly. Then have a child hold up the photo she found. Have that classmate stand and say his name. Collect that photo and have the student sit. Then continue with each remaining photo. *Participating in a game*

Kim Criswell, Wilson Elementary, Wilson, KS

Silent Circle

Little ones communicate through American Sign Language with this fun idea! Teach students to say a familiar word using sign language. After practicing the word with youngsters, engage them in a game of silent circle. To play, sign the word to a child sitting near you and then prompt that child to sign the word to a classmate sitting beside him. Prompt students to continue signing the word around the circle until everyone has had a turn. Then lead youngsters in signing a round of applause! (See the picture shown.) *Communicating with American Sign Language*

Christine Cavin
YMCA of Frederick
Frederick, MD

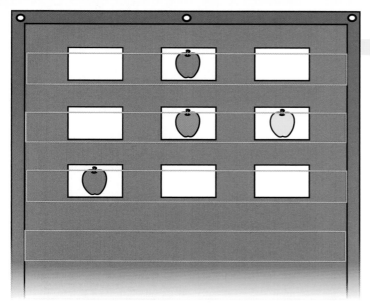

Colorful Apples

Attach red, green, and yellow apple cutouts to index cards. Then place them in a pocket chart with the apples facing away from the viewers. Gather student name sticks (or name cards). To begin, lead students in singing the song. Then choose a stick and read the name. Have the child choose an index card, turn it over, and identify the color of the apple. Continue singing the song and choosing youngsters until all the cards are facing forward. If desired, help students sort the apples by color. *Identifying colors, sorting*

(sung to the tune of "Clementine")

Pick an apple, pick an apple,
Pick an apple from our tree.
Is it green, or is it yellow?
Is it red? Oh, can you see?

Lindsey Bachman, YWCA Early Learning Center, Duluth, MN

The Magic Hat!

Transform an oatmeal container into a top hat as shown. Personalize a white rabbit cutout (see page 37) for each child and then place the cutouts in the hat. Explain that if you say the magic words correctly, a rabbit will appear in the hat. Lead students in saying, "Bippity, hippity, bobbity, hoppity!" Then say, "I think the magic words worked!" Pull out one of the rabbit cutouts and help students read the name on the cutout. Continue pulling out rabbits and having students identify the names, explaining that they must have said the magic words too well because there are lots of rabbits in the hat! *Identifying classmates' names*

Robin Kent
Avon Nursery School
Avon, MA

Circle Time

Mashed Potatoes

Giggles guaranteed!

This positional word activity is sure to elicit lots of giggles! With children seated, hand each child a potato cutout. Say, "Place the potato on your head." Check to see that youngsters followed the direction. Then ask, "Is it mashed yet?" Little ones will surely giggle and reply, "No!" Then continue with other directions that include positional words—such as *behind, in front, on,* and *beside*—followed by the same question. Finally, direct each child to put the potato *under* his bottom and wiggle around. Ask, "Is it mashed yet?" The answer should be a resounding "Yes!"
Understanding positional words

Marie E. Cecchini
West Dundee, IL

Little Leaf Collectors

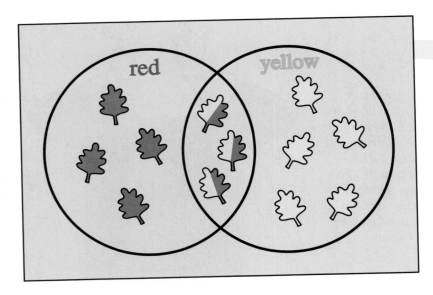

Display a Venn diagram programmed as shown. Gather leaves (or make leaf cutouts) that are red, yellow, and both red and yellow. Then scatter the leaves around the classroom. Direct each of your little leaf collectors to find one leaf and bring it back to her seat. After everyone has returned, invite each child to display her leaf and name its color or colors. Then help her attach her leaf to the diagram. Finally, review with students the information gathered from the diagram. ***Organizing data***

Barbara Moody
Sippican Elementary
Marion, MA

Supersize Web!

Engage youngsters with this twist on a well-known idea! Hand a child a large ball of yarn. Direct her to hold tightly to the loose end of yarn with one hand and then roll the ball to a classmate using her other hand. Instruct that classmate to hold onto the yarn nearest the ball and then roll the ball to another child. Have students repeat the process until each child has had a turn to help "spin" the web. Finally, have a volunteer (bug) "fly" into the middle of the web. Then have his classmates stand and lift the web to trap the bug! *Fine-motor skills*

Kalee Greve, Centered On Kids, Moorhead, MN

Mr. Turkey

Youngsters practice two math skills with this activity and rhyme! Label index cards with numbers and place them in your pocket chart. Hide colorful feather cutouts behind the cards and display a turkey body cutout. Lead youngsters in saying the first verse of the rhyme; then you say the second verse, inserting a child's name and a number where indicated. That child finds the card with the designated number, removes the feather, and identifies the color. After confirming a correct number and color, attach the feather to the turkey, set the card aside, and repeat the process. *Recognizing numbers, identifying colors*

Mr. Turkey, look at you!
You lost your feathers.
What will you do?

[Child's name] can help you, yes sirree!
Look behind [number].
What do you see?

Jennie Jensen
North Cedar Elementary
Lowden, IA

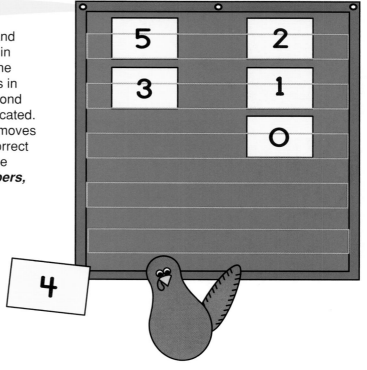

Circle Time

Time to Fly!

Make an oversize masking tape *V* on the floor. Label several goose cutouts (patterns on page 38) with letters, writing *V* on most. Explain that when geese fly, they do so in a *V* shape. First, it makes flying easier by reducing wind resistance. Second, it helps them keep track of every bird in the group. Then display a cutout and have youngsters identify the letter. If the letter is *V*, place the cutout on the masking tape *V*. If the letter is not *V*, set the cutout aside. Repeat with the remaining cutouts. **Letter identification**

Roxanne LaBell Dearman
NC Intervention for the Deaf and Hard of Hearing
Charlotte, NC

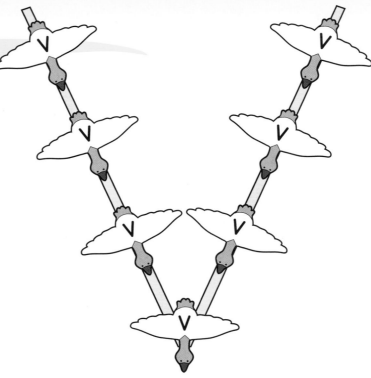

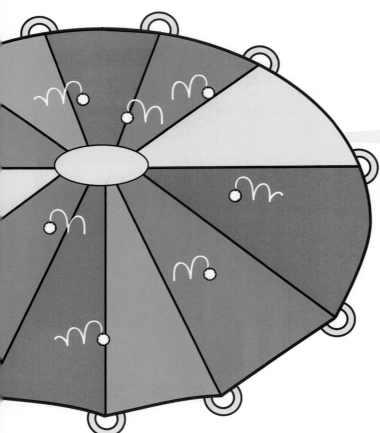

It's Snowing!

Youngsters exercise arm muscles and counting skills with this activity. Have students hold the edge of a parachute (or bedsheet) as you toss a class supply of white pom-poms (snowflakes) onto it. Next, help the group gently shake the parachute as you say the rhyme. Then vigorously shake it until all the snow falls to the ground. When the snowstorm is over, lay the parachute down and instruct each student to pick up one snowflake. Next, prompt each child to toss her snowflake onto the parachute as you lead the class in counting each one aloud. Then create another snowstorm! **Gross-motor skills, counting**

It's getting cold, and the sky is gray—
It looks like we might get snow today!

Karen Eiben
The Learning House Preschool
LaSalle, IL

"Christmas-Pokey"

Youngsters practice *left* and *right* with a familiar tune and a holiday twist! Use green Christmas garland to make an oversize wreath on the floor. If desired, add accents like a big bow and pom-pom berries. Put a holiday sticker on each student's right hand and right foot. Then name either the right or left hand. Play a musical recording while students dance around the wreath. When you stop the music, students put the correct hand in the wreath. Continue in the same way, naming different hands and feet. ***Concept of left and right***

adapted from an idea by Keely Saunders
Bonney Lake Early Childhood Education Assistance Program
Bonney Lake, WA

Dizzy Dreidels

Here's a fun way for little ones to practice identifying the letter *D*! Label several dreidel cutouts with letters, writing *D* on most. Have youngsters stand with lots of space between them. Then display one of the dreidels. If it shows a letter *D*, students say, "*D* is for *dizzy dreidels*!" Then you sing the song as the children slowly spin around, falling down at the end. If the dreidel shows a different letter, youngsters stand quietly. Continue with each remaining dreidel. ***Identifying the letter* D**

(sung to the tune of "Shoo Fly")

Dreidel, spin round and round,
Dreidel, spin round and round,
Dreidel, spin round and round
Until you stop and then fall down!

Roxanne LaBell Dearman
NC Intervention for the Deaf and Hard of Hearing
Charlotte, NC

Circle Time

Spot the Letter

Label several large cards with letters. To play, direct students to close their eyes while you post a card somewhere in the area. Then sing the song shown, prompting youngsters at the end of the song to open their eyes and look for the designated letter. When a child finds it, he calls out, "I spot the letter [letter name]!" Have him point out the letter card. Then repeat the activity, leaving the card in place after each round. To conclude the activity, point to each card and encourage students to identify the letter. *Identifying letters*

(sung to the tune of "Pop! Goes the Weasel")

All around our classroom,
The children look to see.
Can you spot the letter [letter name]?
Find one for me!

Tricia Kylene Brown
Bowling Green, KY

I spot the letter A!

Touching Tune

Have youngsters stand with plenty of space between them; then give each child a heart pointer. (Make sure to have one for yourself!) Lead little ones in performing the song shown. Then repeat the activity with the suggestions below. *Recognizing body parts*

(sung to the tune of "This Old Man")

Touch your [knee] with your heart.
Let's all learn our body parts.
Then we jump, jump, turn around,
Wiggle high and low.
Let's see what else we all know!

Continue with the following: *nose, chin, head, ear, mouth, hip, foot, shin, elbow, shoulder, back, tummy*

Robin Johnson
Cromwell-Wright Public School
Cromwell, MN

Circle Time

> I'd give one to Jordan, that's who.

Flowers for You!

Get a plastic (or real) flower. Explain that flowers are a traditional gift on Valentine's Day. Recite the chant shown, adding a student name where indicated. Then give the flower to the child. Have the child name a classmate. Then prompt youngsters to recite the chant with the new name. Encourage the student to give the flower to that classmate. Continue until everyone gets to hold the flower. ***Participating in a rhyme***

Who would I give a flower to?
I'd give one to [child's name], that's who!

Suzanne Moore
Tucson, AZ

Leaping Leprechauns!

Gather number cards. Then lead students in reciting the rhyme shown, moving as suggested. Next, have a child choose a number card. Help him identify the number. Then prompt students to leap the appropriate number of times. Continue with different number cards. ***Identifying numbers, gross-motor skills***

Leprechauns, leprechauns can't be still—	*Wiggle body.*
Searching high and searching low.	*Hold hand over brow and look high and low.*
Are you near the rainbow's end?	*Move hand in an arc to indicate a rainbow.*
How many leaps must you still go?	*Shake index finger.*

Roxanne LaBell Dearman
NC Intervention for the Deaf and Hard of Hearing
Charlotte, NC

Big Top Hat

Make a large tagboard hat like the one shown. Label the top white stripe "hat" and the remaining white stripes "_at." Gather assorted letter cards. To begin, lead youngsters in reading the word *hat*; then point to the *h* and have students say the letter name and its sound. Next, recite the rhyme shown, displaying a card at the appropriate time and pausing to allow students to name the letter. Then complete the rhyme using the new word. Write the chosen letter in a blank space on the hat and repeat the activity with the remaining cards. After the words are complete, conclude the activity by helping students read them. ***Letter-sound association***

That mischievous cat
Wore a big top hat.
Change the *h* to [letter name]
And the word is [new word]!

Linda Gill
St. Joseph School
Bartlett, IL

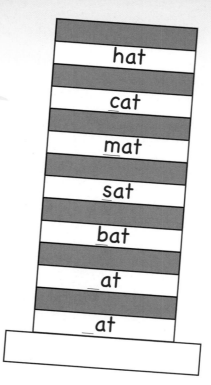

hat
cat
mat
sat
bat
_at
_at

P Is for Peas and...

Pickle!

Encourage youngsters to name words that begin with the /p/ sound after reciting the rhyme "Peas Porridge Hot." Hand a child a small pot containing green pom-poms (peas). Have students pass the pot around the circle as you lead them in saying the traditional rhyme. At the end of the rhyme, prompt the child with the pot to remove a pea and say a word that begins with /p/ like *pea*. Have him return the pea to the pot; then continue the activity for several rounds. ***Beginning sound /p/***

Ada Goren
Winston-Salem, NC

Circle Time

Colorful Spill

Gather a supply of pom-poms in several different colors. Label a class supply of lunch bags with color words in matching colors. To begin, review each color word and its color. Then give each child a bag, recite the chant shown, and spill the pom-poms onto the floor. Prompt each child holding a bag labeled with the designated color word to pick up pom-poms of that color and put them in his bag. Then repeat the chant, inserting a different color name each time until all the pom-poms are picked up. *Recognizing colors, identifying color words*

Fuzzy pom-poms all around,
Pick the [color] ones from the ground!

Donna Ream
Ms. Donna's Daycare
Plainfield, IL

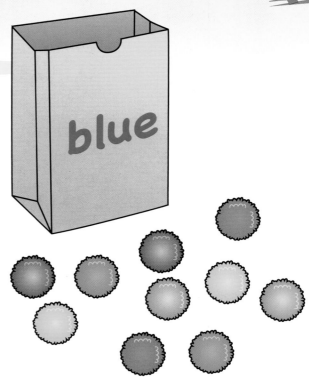

Puddle Jumpers

Cut apart a copy of the first column of cards on page 39 and attach each one to a different puddle cutout. Cut apart extra copies of the cards in the remaining column so each student has one. Then place the puddles on the floor and give a card to each child. Play some music and encourage little ones to dance around the puddles. Stop the music and prompt each child to jump by the nearest puddle. Then have each child say the picture word on the puddle and on her card to see if the two words rhyme. If they do, she stays by the puddle. If they do not, she steps away from the puddle. Lead youngsters in a round of applause for a job well done; then restart the music! *Rhyming*

Kelly Ash
Waukesha, WI

A Tisket, a Tasket

Conceal a different letter tile in each of several plastic eggs; then place the eggs in a handled basket. Give a child the basket and have him walk around the inside of the circle as you lead the group in singing the song shown. At the end of the song, prompt the child to drop an egg in the lap of the nearest classmate. Have the classmate open the egg and identify the letter; then set the egg aside and choose a different child to walk with the basket. Continue until the basket is empty. *Identifying letters*

(sung to the tune of "A Tisket, a Tasket")

A tisket, a tasket,
I'm walking with my basket
Filled with eggs for my friends.
But on the way, I lost one!

adapted from an idea by Janet Boyce, Cokato, MN

Butterfly Bubbles

Popping bubbles is lots of fun, but catching one can be quite a challenge! Have children stand with plenty of space between them; then display a bottle of bubbles. Ask youngsters to imagine that the bubbles you are about to blow are delicate butterflies fluttering through the air. Then blow some bubbles and challenge each student to gently catch one in her hands. *Participating in a group activity*

Aimee Robertson
School for Little People
Sherman, TX

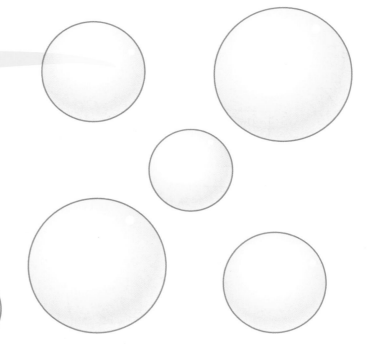

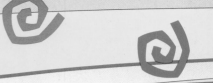

Circle Time

Pretty Little Butterfly

Help students practice body awareness and exercise their muscles! Have each child attach a construction paper rectangle to a craft stick and bend the paper slightly as shown (butterfly). Have youngsters wiggle their props back and forth to make the butterflies flutter. Then recite the rhyme shown, prompting students to move their butterflies as indicated and then to make the butterflies land on the designated body part. Repeat the rhyme, inserting a different body part each time. **Body awareness, gross-motor skills**

Pretty little butterfly,
Flying low and flying high,
Landed on my [body part]
And then flew into the sky!

Elizabeth Cook
St. Louis, MO

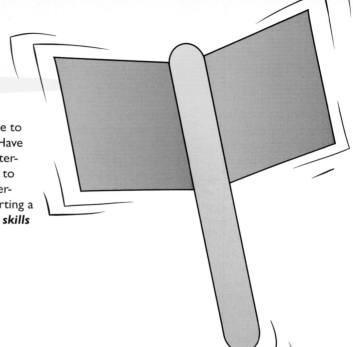

At the Pond

Little ones need their thinking caps for this pond-related activity! Have youngsters stand around the edge of a large pond-shaped cutout (or a blue blanket). Then tell them to listen carefully as you recite the rhyme shown. If the critter named lives in the pond, have the child jump into the pond. If the critter lives out of the pond, have a child sit down where he is. If the animal likes to be in and out of the pond, the child sits down so part of him is in the pond and part of him is out. Continue with the suggested critters. **Activating prior knowledge, gross-motor skills**

I might stay in. I might stay out.
But being a [fish] is what I'm about!

Kimberli Usselman
Victor, NY

Suggested critters: duck, frog, turtle (in and out); dragonfly, bird, deer (out); tadpole, crayfish (in)

Circle Time

Packed and Ready

Get youngsters excited about summer vacation plans with this beginning sound review. Cover a cardboard box with old maps. Then place in the box items you might pack for a vacation, such as a bathing suit, a hat, a camera, or sunglasses. Set the box in the center of the circle-time area and then lead youngsters in reciting the rhyme shown. At the end of the rhyme, invite a child to take an item from the box, name it, and say its beginning sound. If desired, conclude the activity by encouraging volunteers to tell about their summer vacation plans. **Beginning sounds**

I'm going on vacation.
I'm so happy I could sing.
Let's look inside my suitcase
To see what I might bring.

Linda Rasberry
Park Avenue Christian Academy
Titusville, FL

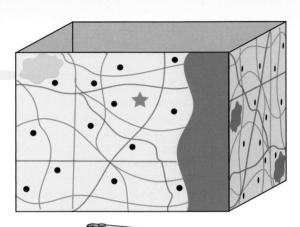

Syllable Sort

Youngsters will applaud this low-prep activity! Gather a collection of classroom objects whose names have one to three syllables. Set the objects near a length of bulletin board paper labeled as shown. Invite a volunteer to choose an item and show it to his classmates. Lead youngsters in clapping the number of syllables in the object's name. Then have the child place it on the correct section of the chart. After completing the activity, place the chart and objects at a center for individual practice. **Counting syllables**

Heather Cohen
Sunlight Christian Academy
Port Saint Lucie, FL

Puppet Parade

Number five self-adhesive nametags from 1 to 5. Then attach each nametag to a different hand puppet. Invite five volunteers to each wear a puppet. Then have them line up in the correct order for the puppet parade. Guide the seated students in checking the order of the puppets. If the order is correct, invite the youngsters holding puppets to parade around the circle-time area. (For extra fun, play upbeat music for the parade!) If the order is not correct, have the students holding puppets correct their order before beginning the parade. Continue for several rounds. **Number order**

Tricia Kylene Brown
Bowling Green, KY

O is for ocean!

O Is for Ocean

Name an animal. If the animal lives in the ocean, prompt little ones to raise their arms so they look like a giant *O* and say, "*O* is for *ocean!*" If the animal does not live in the ocean, students stand still. Continue with a variety of animals. **Investigating living things, letter-sound association**

adapted from an idea by Lindsay Faller
Kid Kollege
Mesa, AZ

Circle Time

Alphabet Walk

Scatter letter cards or die-cut letters in the center of your circle-time area. Then lead youngsters in singing the "Alphabet Song" as they walk around the letters. When the song ends, invite a child to pick up a letter. Sing the song a second time, encouraging each child to hold up his letter when it is named in the song. Have students return the letters and play another round. ***Recognizing letters***

Shelli Hurlocker
Busy Bees Christian Preschool
Kokomo, IN

What will you grow in your [picture] ?

Maybe [corn] it grows so tall.

Maybe [beets] I will pick them all.

Maybe [potatoes] I will dig deep down.

Maybe [squash] so giant and round.

But one thing that will surely grow:

Weeds! I'll pull them row by row.

Vegetable Garden

What kinds of yummy things grow in a garden during the summer? Youngsters find out as they read this rhyme. Use programmed sentence strips and a cut-apart copy of the picture cards on page 40 to prepare the rebus rhyme shown. To reinforce tracking print, invite a volunteer to point to the words and pictures as you lead the group in reading the rhyme. If desired, use the rhyme to review other concepts, such as letter recognition or spacing between words. After students become familiar with the rhyme, invite them to add movements to each line to create an entertaining performance.

Elizabeth Cook
Glendale Lutheran ELC
Glendale, MO

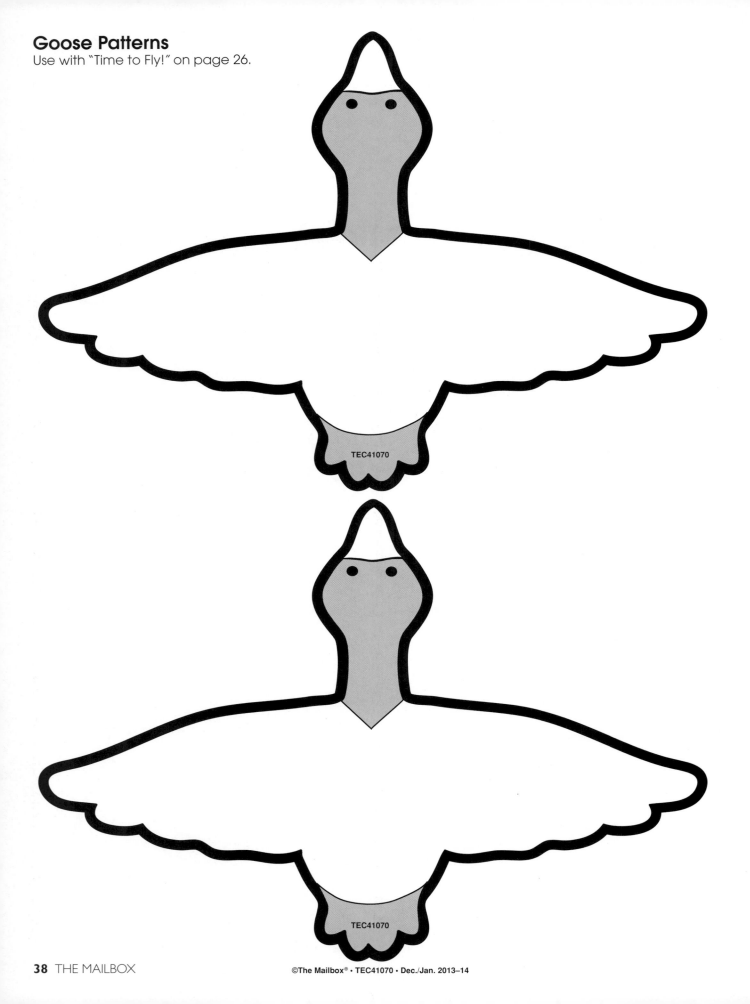

TEC41070

TEC41070

TEC41072

TEC41072

TEC41072

TEC41072

TEC41072

TEC41072

TEC41072

TEC41072

Picture Cards

Use with "Vegetable Garden" on page 36.

TEC41073

TEC41073

TEC41073

TEC41073

TEC41073

Classroom Displays

"Hoppy" Birthday!

Scott
June 20th

Mia
January 13th

Kelly
March 23rd

Adam
May 15th

Lauren
September 10th

Darrell
November 19th

Have each child color a copy of the frog pattern on page 48. Encourage her to spread glue on the cupcake and then sprinkle confetti on the glue. Display the frogs on lily pad cutouts labeled with youngsters' names and birthdates along with the details and title shown.

Debbie Jourdanis, Argyle Village Nursery School, Argyle, NY

Blue Stuff!

Spiral PASTA

This oversize collage is perfect for identifying colors and developing vocabulary! Send a bag home with each youngster along with a note encouraging parents to help their child choose items in a particular color to bring to school. Possible items include very small toys, magazine pictures, and food labels. Attach the items to a board and add a title. Discuss youngsters' contributions to the display and then use the display to play "I Spy."

Kila Atcheson
Cumming First United Methodist Church Preschool
Cumming, GA

CLASSROOM DISPLAYS

This Classroom Community Is Warm and Cozy!

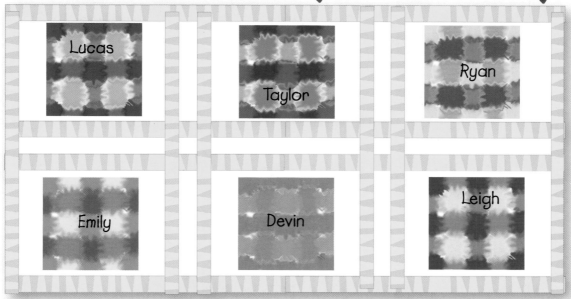

Build a cozy classroom community with this handmade quilt project! Give each child a white paper towel that's been folded several times. Have her apply brightly tinted water to the towel using an eyedropper; then unfold the towel for quick drying. Display the towels and add quilt details with crepe paper or colored tape.

Joanne Baugh, Giggly Wiggly Preschool, Sammamish, WA

To make a jack-o'-lantern lollipop, have each child tape a straw to a small paper plate. Help him wrap the resulting lollipop in orange cellophane and tie curling ribbon around it. Then invite him to add construction paper facial features. Mount the lollipops on a board or wall with the title shown.

Kathleen Majewski
Penfield Village Nursery School and Kindergarten
Penfield, NY

Pint-Size Penguins!

To make this cute penguin display, paint the bottom edge of each child's foot black, leaving the middle unpainted (stomach); then paint his toes orange. Have him press his foot onto white construction paper. To make wings, help him add a black toe print on either side. Then have him add eye and beak cutouts to the print. When the paint is dry, trim around each print and display it as shown.

Lisa Frazier, Footsteps & Fingerprints, Bonham, TX
Bridget Williamson, Bridget's Childcare, Sewell, NJ

We Love
the Holidays!

You'll love this sweet holiday display! Have each child paint stripes on two candy cane cutouts. Then glue the candy canes together so they resemble a heart. Attach the projects to a board decorated as shown and then mount a picture of each child in the middle of his project.

Theresa Wensil
Tiny Tears Daycare
Albemarle, NC

CLASSROOM DISPLAYS

Windy, windy weather,
Can you feel the breeze?
It lifts your coat and flips your hair
And rustles through the trees.

For each child, cut the bottom from a lunch-size paper bag. Then have her color the bag as desired and attach a construction paper handle and crepe paper strips to create a windsock. Attach the windsocks to a board so they appear to be blowing in the breeze. Then attach the poem shown along with clouds cut from quilt batting.

Mandi Ellis
Primrose School
Ashburn, VA

For a twist on the name "Mt. Rushmore," incorporate the name of your school! This display is named "Mt. Brightmore" in reference to Bright Beginnings, the school at which our idea contributor works.

Mt. Brightmore

Presidents' Day is February 17! Why not celebrate it with this grin-inducing display. To begin, show youngsters a photo of Mt. Rushmore and explain that the faces of four presidents are carved in the rock. Have students color brown craft paper with brown unwrapped crayons. Then encourage them to crumple the paper. Staple the paper to a board so it resembles a mountain. Then attach sepia-tone photos of youngsters' heads to the mountain.

Jennifer Joyce, Bright Beginnings, Southington, CT

CLASSROOM DISPLAYS

Mirror, Mirror on the Wall, We Love Our Moms Best of All!

Youngsters engage in a labor of love to make this cute Mother's Day display! For each child, lightly pencil the words shown on a tagboard rectangle. Have her trace the words with a glitter pen and then attach a craft foam heart with her photo between the words. Punch two holes at the top and add a ribbon hanger. Mount the projects around an aluminum foil "mirror" as shown.

Dana Vierno, Nursery Rhymes, Saddle Brook, NJ

This display is a perfect reminder to help keep our earth clean! To make a litterbug, have each child glue clean trash or recyclable items to a tagboard semicircle (body). Have him glue head, leg, and antenna cutouts to the body. Display the litterbugs with trash can and recycling bin cutouts.

Lisa Hester
Tendercare Learning Centers
Pittsburgh, PA

CLASSROOM DISPLAYS

An Underwater Ocean View!

All hands and arms are on deck to make the coral for this ocean display! Invite each child to press a painted forearm, palm, and fingers (coral) near the bottom of a sheet of bulletin board paper decorated to look like the ocean floor. Then encourage her to add colorful fingerprint details to the coral and ocean critter drawings to the scene.

Toni Chambers, First Baptist Jensen Beach Preschool, Jensen Beach, FL

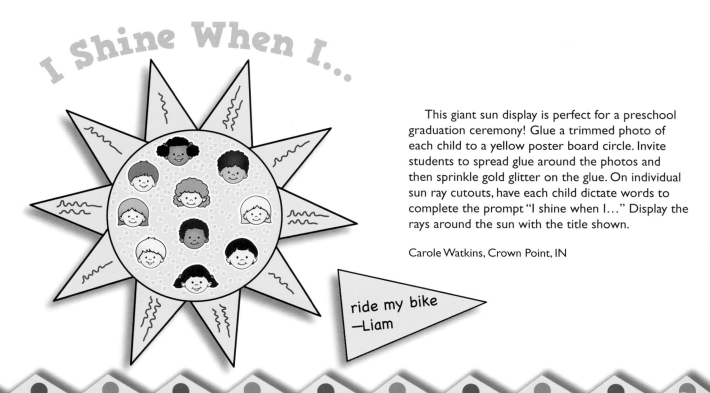

I Shine When I...

ride my bike
—Liam

This giant sun display is perfect for a preschool graduation ceremony! Glue a trimmed photo of each child to a yellow poster board circle. Invite students to spread glue around the photos and then sprinkle gold glitter on the glue. On individual sun ray cutouts, have each child dictate words to complete the prompt "I shine when I..." Display the rays around the sun with the title shown.

Carole Watkins, Crown Point, IN

Frog Pattern
Use with "'Hoppy' Birthday!" on page 42.

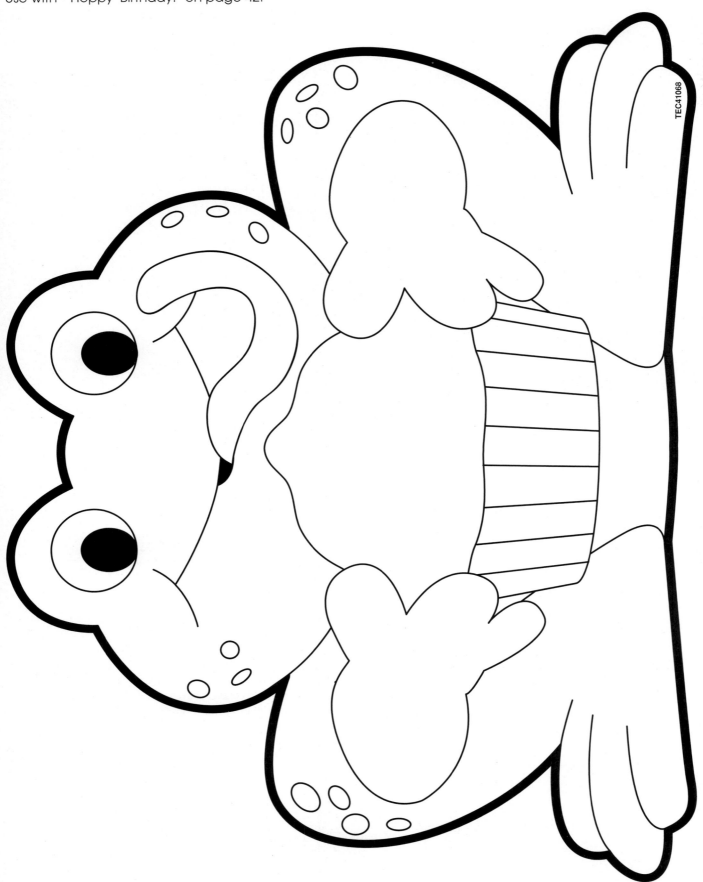

TEC41068

Instant Seasonal Activities

Instant Seasonal Activities

Apple Picking!

Draw an apple tree with many apples on a sheet of chart paper. Recite the rhyme shown. Then ask a child if he would pick one, two, or three apples. Have him cross out the appropriate number of apples on the tree. Continue with different youngsters, reciting the rhyme each time, until all the apples have been picked. **Kate Hogenson, Preschools of St. Andrew's, Mahtomedi, MN**

Apples, apples on the tree,
Pick one, pick one, two or three.
One for you and one for me,
Apples are so yummy!

Tap a Color

Place crayons in a gift bag. Then have a child choose a crayon, look around the room, and then gently tap the crayon on something that is a matching color. Direct him to put the crayon back in the bag. Then repeat the process with another child.

Tall and Short Letters

Gather student name cards and have youngsters notice that some letters—such as *d*, *h*, *l*, and *b*—are tall and reach the top line, but other letters—like *s*, *m*, *a*, and *c*—are short and only touch the middle line. Hold up a name card and then name and point to each letter, having youngsters stand tall for the tall letters and crouch down to the floor for the short letters.

> Analyse

> Jacob

Crisscross Applesauce!

Have students sit with their legs out in front of them. Gather letter cards, including several letter *A*s. Flip through the cards, helping youngsters look for *A*s. When they see one, they cross their legs and say, "Crisscross applesauce!" Then they unfold their legs for the next card.

Super Crayon Center!

Bundle crayons, making sure to put differing numbers of crayons in the sets. Then place them at a center with a variety of paper. Encourage students to explore with the bundled crayons.

Instant Seasonal Activities

Life of a Leaf
Understanding characteristics of the seasons
Have youngsters curl up tightly on the floor as if pretending to be tiny leaves. Then say, "The little leaves begin to grow." Have youngsters stand and stretch out as they pretend to be big leaves. Then say, "The spring breezes blow" as little ones sway back and forth like fluttering leaves. Have them pantomime leaves in a rainstorm, through the heat of summer, during chilly fall nights, and then falling from the trees. For a grand finale, pretend to rake up all your little leaves! What fun!

A Patch of Rhymes
Recognizing rhymes
Name one of the word pairs given. Have a child decide if the words rhyme. If they do, have her use an orange bingo dauber to make a print (pumpkin) on a sheet of chart paper. Continue in the same way until each child has added a pumpkin. Then draw green vines on the page so it resembles a pumpkin patch!

fall, ball	chill, fly
run, pack	yellow, fellow
leaf, reef	oak, spoke
sweater, better	tree, see
rake, bake	patch, match
pile, tile	corn, horn
red, bed	gourd, board
brown, down	crow, mow

I Spy a Color
Recognizing colors
Gather a fall-themed book, such as *Fall Leaves Fall!* by Zoe Hall. Open the book to a random page and note one of the colors shown in the illustration. Say, "I spy [color name]." Then have a child point to the color in the illustration. Continue in the same way, changing colors and illustrations.

Harvesttime!
Representing subtraction with objects
Place ten colorful pom-poms (fall crops) on the floor. Have youngsters help you count the crops. Say, "[Child's name] picked some corn." Have the child remove one pom-pom. Then have students count the remaining pom-poms. Continue in the same way, one at a time, until all the crops have been picked.

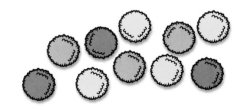

For Thanksgiving Day dinner, I would make...

turkey · pizza · cake

What's on Your Plate?
Writing
Encourage youngsters to describe their ideal Thanksgiving Day dinner with this simple idea! Give a child a noncoated paper plate. Then tell her to pretend she is making Thanksgiving Day dinner for her friends. Have her draw what she would make on the plate. Then help her label her drawings as shown.

Got Your Nose!
Participating in a rhyme

Recite the traditional rhyme shown with your youngsters. Then ask, "What if the snowman had a banana nose? Who would want to eat it?" Encourage youngsters to conclude that a monkey would want the nose. Then repeat the rhyme, substituting *banana* and *monkey* appropriately. Continue with the following: *acorn/squirrel*, *bone/puppy*, and *ice cream cone/child*. What fun!
Terri Vrasich, Noah's Ark Preschool, McHenry, IL

A chubby little snowman
Had a [carrot] nose.
Along came a [bunny],
And what do you suppose?
The hungry little [bunny],
Looking for its lunch,
Ate that snowman's [carrot] nose—
Nibble, nibble crunch!

Snowflake Cleanup
Gross-motor skills

Divide youngsters into two groups and give white pom-poms (snowflakes) to every child in one group (Team 1). Place empty tubs nearby. Play a musical recording and encourage Team 1 to toss the snowflakes on the ground. Team 2 cleans up the snowflakes by placing them in the tubs. But Team 1 can remove them from the tubs and put them back on the ground! As play continues, randomly stop the music. The team with the most snowflakes either cleaned up or scattered on the floor is declared the winner. **Sandra Ratcliff, Simonsdale Presbyterian Preschool, Portsmouth, VA**

Hats and Mittens
Fine-motor skills

String a piece of clothesline from one chair to another and provide clothespins. Have children place their hats and mittens near the line. Youngsters get a fine-motor workout from hanging the hats and mittens! **Nicole Anast, Plymouth Children's Center, Burlington, WI**

Jingle, Jingle!
Identifying letters, following directions

Give several children jingle-bell bracelets. Gather letter cards and tuck several simple bell cards into the mix. Hold up the cards one at a time and help students identify the letters. When a bell card is revealed, prompt students to play their bells.

Instant Seasonal Activities

I'm a Love Bug!
Participating in a fingerplay
Youngsters will love this quick little fingerplay!

I am a love bug.	*Link thumbs.*
I fly like this.	*Wiggle fingers.*
What do I do?	*Throw arms outward.*
I kiss, kiss, kiss!	*Bunch fingers on both hands and tap them together.*

Ada Goren, Lewisville, NC

Colorful Sheep!
Identifying colors
Gather colorful pom-poms, making sure there are three of each color. Place the pom-poms in a container. Have a child choose a pom-pom and identify the color. Then encourage him to find the other pom-poms that match. Next, help him sing the familiar song shown, substituting the appropriate color word.

Baa, baa, [color word] sheep,
Have you any wool?
Yes, sir; yes, sir; three bags full!

Karen Guess

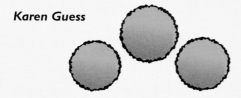

With a Lion or a Lamb?
Investigating living things, categorizing
Explain that lions live in the grasslands of Africa and lambs live on a farm. Then name another animal that might live in one of the locations, such as a zebra or a goat. If the animal named would live with a lion, prompt students to roar, and if it would live with a lamb, have students baa. Continue with other animals.

Like a Kite
Gross-motor skills
Ask, "Have you ever seen a kite?" After students share their experiences, invite youngsters to move like kites. Then ask them to brainstorm other things that might be found in the air, like birds, bugs, airplanes, and helicopters. Prompt students to move like each item named. ***Karen Guess, IUPUI Center for Young Children, Indianapolis, IN***

Leprechaun's Beard
Speaking
Draw a simple leprechaun on your board. Ask a child a question, such as "What would you do with a leprechaun's gold?" or "How would you catch a leprechaun?" After he answers the question, encourage him to draw a curlicue on the leprechaun. Continue asking youngsters questions until the leprechaun has a full beard.

Cotton Ball Race
Oral-motor skills
Place two cotton balls at one end of a table. Give each of two children a straw. Then prompt the students to blow the cotton balls to the opposite end of the table using the straws. Repeat with other pairs of students. ***Connie Childs-Massingill, Dawn 'til Dusk Daycare, Zionsville, IN***

Instant Seasonal Activities

Spring Sounds
Creating sound and action patterns
Write different spring themes on your board. Then have students help you come up with a sound and action for each item. For example, for rain, youngsters might say, "plop," as they hit the floor with their hands; for frogs, they might say, "ribbit," as they hop; and for birds, they might say, "tweet," as they flap their arms. Then guide students in creating patterns using the sounds and actions, such as "plop, ribbit, plop, ribbit..."

Rain Daubers
Recognizing beginning sound /r/
Say a word. If the word begins with /r/, a child uses a blue bingo dauber to make a mark (raindrop) on a sheet of chart paper. Continue with other words (see the suggestions shown) until the paper is covered with raindrops!

Suggested words: *rope, rose, rug, whale, ring, rip, saw, right, zip, ram, ball, rat, dot, rule, real, tube, raccoon, rocket, ribbon, cat, roll, round, red, read, fan, road, rock, radish*

Don't Melt the Egg!
Participating in a game, gross-motor skills
Shape brown play dough so it resembles a chocolate egg and seat youngsters in a circle. Then have students sing the song shown as they quickly pass the egg around the circle. When the song is finished, the child with the egg gives it to his neighbor and then hops like a bunny to the middle of the circle. Continue with another round of the game!

(sung to the tune of "O Christmas Tree")

Our hands are warm. Our hands are warm.
Please do not melt the chocolate!
Our hands are warm. Our hands are warm.
Please do not melt the chocolate!
It might get sticky—messy too!
And then the egg will just be goo!
Our hands are warm. Our hands are warm.
Please do not melt the chocolate!

Count and Move
Identifying numbers, counting, naming animal babies
Have little ones name a baby animal and then discuss ways the animal moves. For example, a duckling might flap its wings or waddle. Next, place a deck of cards face-down. A child chooses a card and identifies the number on the card. Then youngsters perform a specified animal action that many times. What a fun and simple game!
Roxanne LaBell Dearman, NC Intervention for the Deaf and Hard of Hearing, Charlotte, NC

KIDS IN THE KITCHEN

Kids in the Kitchen

These self-likenesses will be as unique as your students. Encourage each youngster to use a desired combination of vegetables to create his masterpiece. Then dip the pieces in salad dressing. Yum!

Edible Self-Portraits

Ingredients for one:
thinly sliced pepper strips
thinly sliced cucumber rounds
thinly sliced cherry tomato slices
sugar snap peas
julienned carrots
light salad dressing in a cup

Jodi G. Zeis
Elgin, SC

Supplies:
paper plate

Teacher preparation:
Arrange the ingredients and supplies near a colored copy of the step-by-step recipe cards (see page 57).

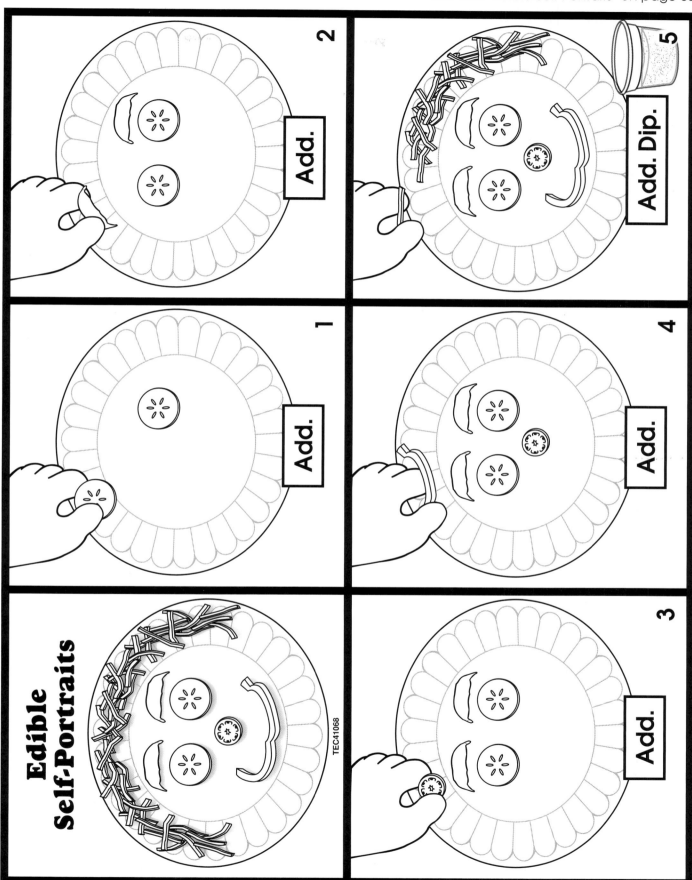

Edible Self-Portraits

2 Add.

1 Add.

Add. Dip. 5

4 Add.

3 Add.

TEC41068

Kids in the Kitchen

This yummy treat makes the perfect snack for any fall celebration.

Personal Pumpkin Dip

Ingredients for one:
pumpkin pie filling
whipped cream cheese
thinly sliced apples
gingersnaps

Utensils and supplies:
resealable plastic bag
plastic spoons
paper plate
scissors

Teacher preparation:
Arrange the ingredients and supplies near a colored copy of the step-by-step recipe cards (see page 59).

Jodi G. Zeis
Elgin, SC

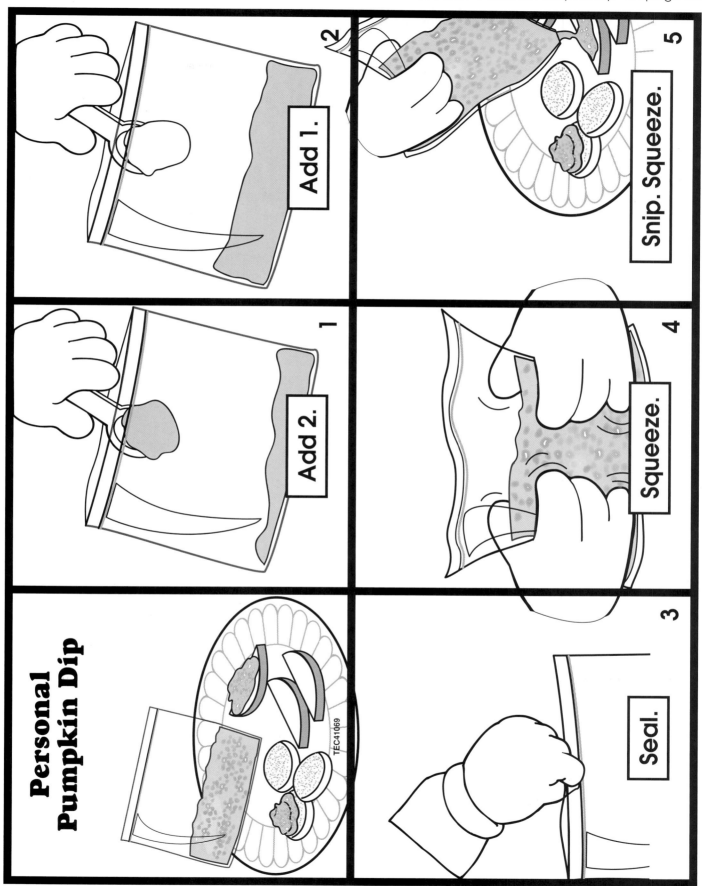

Add 1.

2

Add 2.

1

Snip. Squeeze.

5

Squeeze.

4

Seal.

3

Personal Pumpkin Dip

TEC41069

Kids in the Kitchen

This healthy treat is perfect for your holiday celebration!

Tasty Trees

Ingredients for one:
slice of bread
green-tinted whipped cream cheese
broccoli (finely chopped)
red pepper (finely chopped)
thin piece of celery

Utensils and supplies:
paper plate
plastic knife

Teacher preparation:
Arrange the ingredients and supplies near a colored copy of the step-by-step recipe cards (see page 61).

Jodi G. Zeis
Elgin, SC

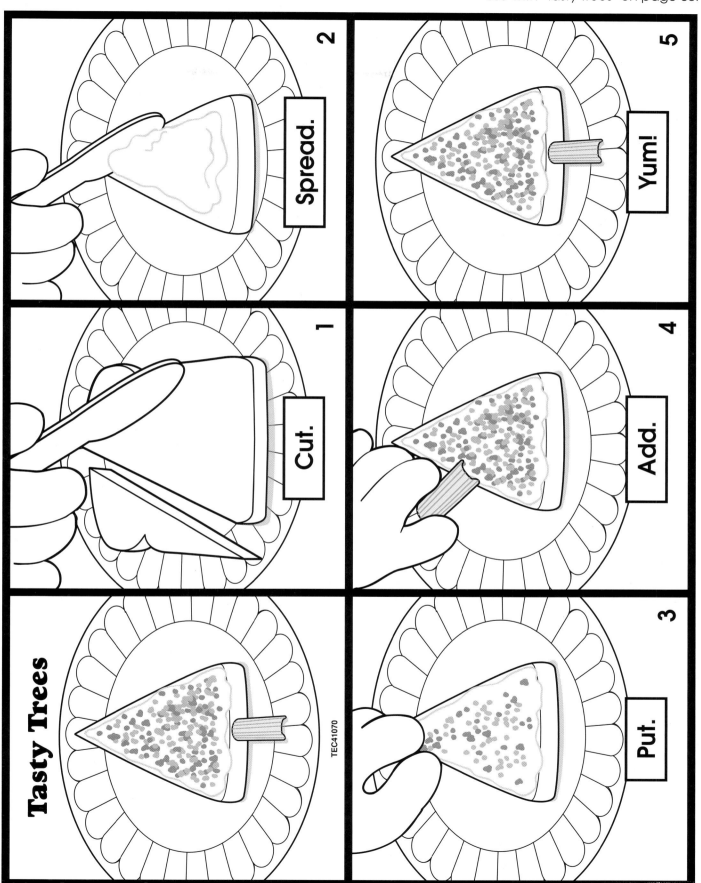

2 Spread.

5 Yum!

1 Cut.

4 Add.

Tasty Trees

TEC41070

3 Put.

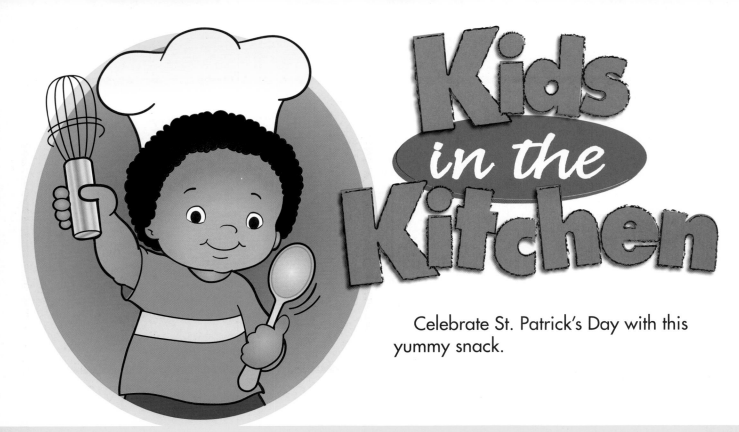

Kids in the Kitchen

Celebrate St. Patrick's Day with this yummy snack.

Rainbow Cups

Ingredients for one:
red-tinted vanilla pudding
yellow-tinted vanilla pudding
blue-tinted vanilla pudding
vanilla wafer cookies (gold coins)

Lisa Igou
Silbernagel Elementary
Dickinson, TX

Utensils and supplies:
clear plastic cup
plastic spoons
resealable plastic bag

Teacher preparation:
Arrange the ingredients and supplies near a colored copy of the step-by-step recipe cards (see page 63).

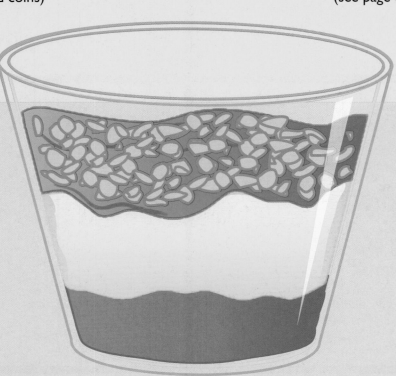

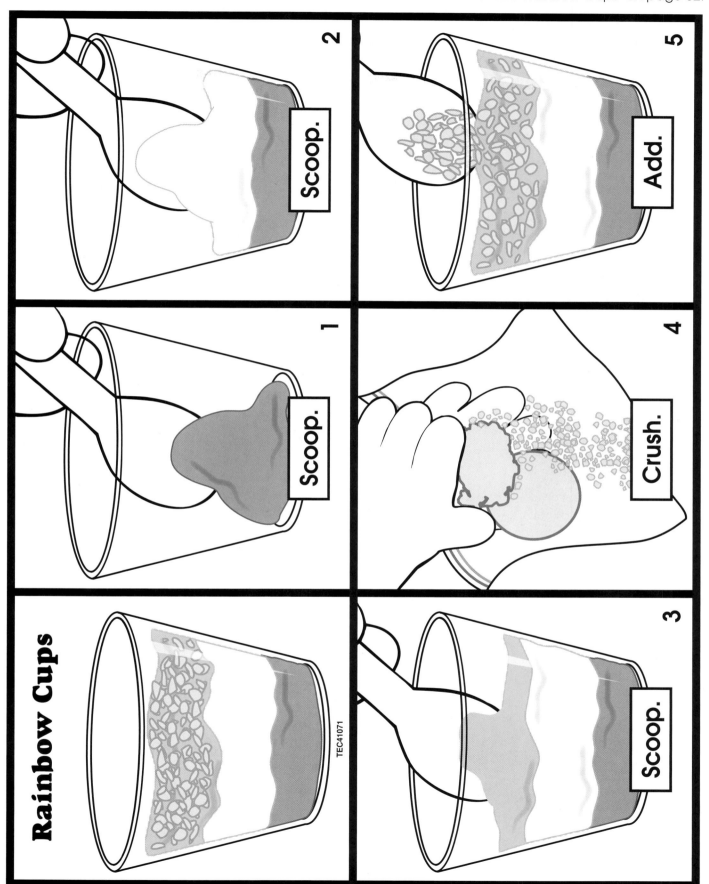

Rainbow Cups

2 · Scoop.

1 · Scoop.

5 · Add.

4 · Crush.

3 · Scoop.

TEC41071

Kids in the Kitchen

This simple snack is the perfect springtime treat.

Fancy Flowers

Ingredients for one:
slice of bread
pink-tinted cream cheese
thin banana slice

Utensils and supplies:
flower-shaped cookie cutter
paper plate
plastic knife

Teacher preparation:
Arrange the ingredients and supplies near a colored copy of the step-by-step recipe cards (see page 65).

Janel Kresl
Washington Elementary
Crookston, MN

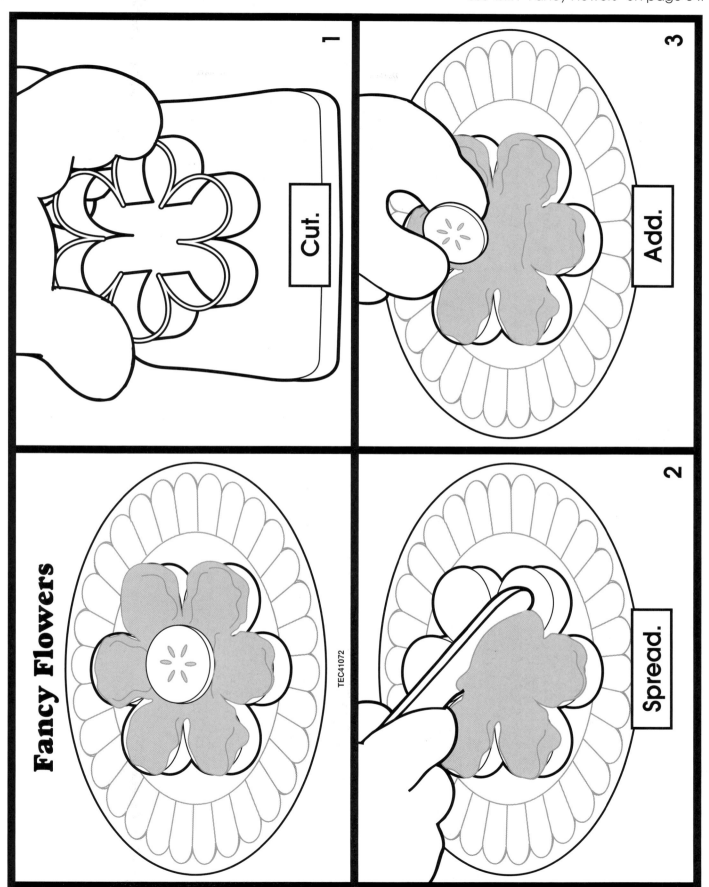

Kids in the Kitchen

This treat is a yummy way to conclude an animal unit or a trip to the zoo!

Alligator Punch

Ingredients for one:
lime sherbet
lemon-lime soda

Utensils and supplies:
clear plastic cup
large spoon

Teacher preparation:
Arrange the ingredients and supplies near a colored copy of the step-by-step recipe cards on page 67.

Susan Flener
Children's Circle
Indianapolis, IN

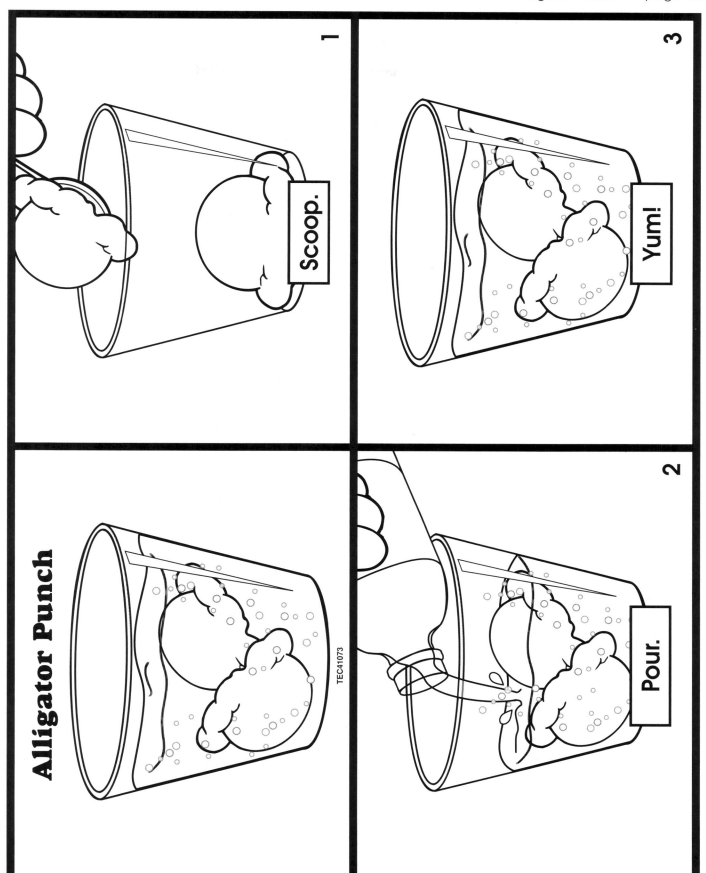

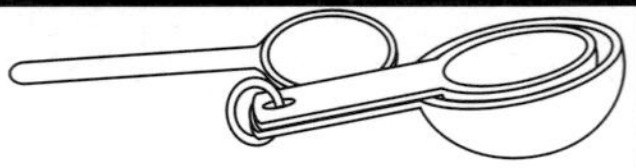

Recipe:_____

From:_____

_____

_____

_____

_____

_____

©The Mailbox®

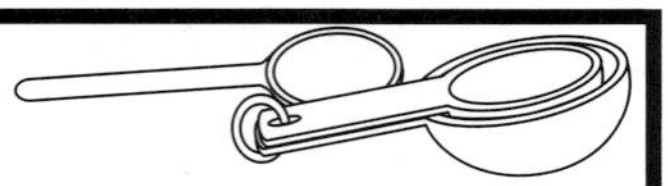

Recipe:_____

From:_____

_____

_____

_____

_____

_____

©The Mailbox®

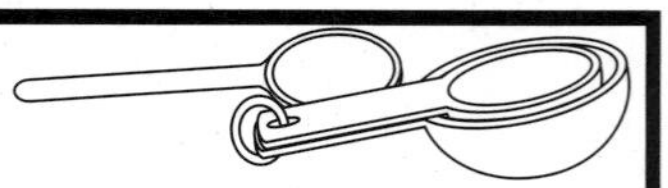

Recipe:_____

From:_____

_____

_____

_____

_____

_____

©The Mailbox®

LEARNING CENTERS

Learning Centers

Apple I Spy
Fine-Motor Area

Tape an apple shape cut from clear Con-Tact covering, sticky-side out, to a flat surface like a wall or an easel. Provide a variety of red, green, and yellow craft items, such as pom-poms, paper squares, yarn pieces, and craft foam shapes. Youngsters visit the center and press the items on the apple, covering its surface. *Fine-motor skills*

Penny Brown
Little Red Schoolhouse
Salem, OR

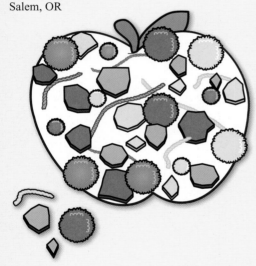

Super Spongy
Art Center

For this process art activity, cover a tabletop with a length of white paper. Set out shallow containers of paint in assorted colors. For each color, provide a different textured sponge, such as a cellulose sponge, an abrasive sponge, and a natural sea sponge. A student dips a sponge in paint and presses it on the paper. He examines the print and then repeats the process with other sponges and colors of paint. His classmates visit the center and repeat the process to make a colorful wall mural with textured designs. *Expressing oneself through art*

Tricia Kylene Brown
Bowling Green, KY

Wormy Apples
Math Center

Laminate several apple cutouts and then punch a different number of holes in each one. Cut green pipe cleaners (worms) in half and place the pieces at the center. A child chooses an apple and counts the holes. Next, she counts the same number of worms and pushes a worm through each hole. She then removes the worms and repeats the process with a different apple. *One-to-one correspondence, counting*

Janet Boyce
Cokato, MN

Learning Centers

Speech Bubbles!
Writing Center

Show little ones how important their words are by showcasing them in speech bubbles! Set out paper, crayons or markers, and a glue stick. Also provide a speech bubble cutout for each child. Invite each student to draw a self-portrait. When he's finished, say, "Now, tell me something about you." Then write his words on a speech bubble and help him glue it to the page. These self-portraits make an adorable display! *Dictating information*

Carole Watkins
Timothy Ball Elementary
Crown Point, IN

G Is for *Garbage*
Literacy Center

Label a small plastic trash can with the word "Garbage." Then place the can on a tabletop. Also label pieces of scrap paper with letters, making sure that many of the letters are *G*s. Crumple the scraps and scatter them near the trash can. A youngster visits the center, chooses a scrap, and smooths it out. If the scrap reveals a *G*, she crumples it up again and tosses it into the trash can. If it reveals another letter, she sets the paper aside. *Recognizing letter* G

Karin Bulkow
Washington School for Comprehensive Literacy
Sheboygan, WI

Foil Rubbing
Discovery Center

Attach to a tray mostly flat objects with familiar shapes, such as a craft foam animal, a die-cut star, a car stencil, and a real or silk leaf. Cover the items with a sheet of heavy duty aluminum foil and place the tray at a center. A child gently rubs his fingers across the foil. As each hidden item's shape appears through the foil, he guesses the object. After rubbing the entire surface of the foil, he removes it from the tray to see if his guesses are correct. *Visual discrimination*

Karen Eiben
LaSalle, IL

Learning Centers

Match a Patch
Math Center

Here's a fun way for little ones to practice making equal sets. Place sets of mini orange pom-poms (pumpkins) in the top row of an ice cube tray. Provide a container of extra pumpkins. A child counts the pumpkins in a section. Then she counts out a matching set of pumpkins and places it in the section below. She continues with each remaining section. ***Making equal sets***

Donna Ream
Ms. Donna's Daycare
Plainfield, IL

Very Hungry Spiders
Science Center

Give each child one paper circle and eight rectangles (spider body and legs). Provide paper, magazines, markers, scissors, and glue. Explain that spiders mainly eat insects, but that some larger spiders will sometimes eat tadpoles, small frogs, fish, birds, or mice! Then have him use the supplies to make a spider. Say, "Your spider looks *very* hungry! What do you think it will eat?" Encourage him to draw or cut out a picture of something his spider might eat and glue it to the spider. If desired, display the spiders with fake spiderwebs and add the title "The Very Hungry Spiders!" ***Investigating living things***

Lisa Shelton
Paragon, IN

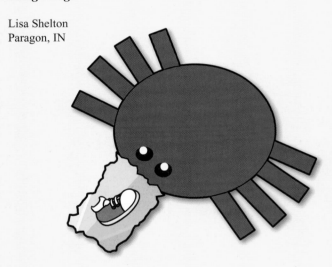

Make a Monster
Games Center

Get a cube-shaped box and make two copies of the monster patterns on page 80. Use one copy to transform the box into a die showing the eyes, the mouth, a horn, an arm, or a foot on five of the sides. Label the remaining side "Roll again!" Cut out the patterns from the remaining copy; then cut apart the monster as shown. Students take turns rolling the die and assembling the monster. When a body part is rolled that is no longer in play, the child's turn ends. When a player rolls "Roll again!" he takes another turn. Play continues until the monster is assembled. ***Participating in a game***

Doria Owen
William Paca Old Post Road Elementary
Abingdon, MD

Hauling Corn
Sensory Center

Partially fill your sensory table with cracked feed corn (or, for younger preschoolers, cornmeal). Add assorted toy farm animals and people along with a toy pickup truck or dump truck. Also provide an empty container (feed bin) and a small plastic shovel or scooper. A child loads the truck with corn feed, hauls it to the feed bin, and then dumps it in. She repeats the process until the feed bin is full, and then she pretends to feed the animals. *Exploring the senses*

Mary Fowler
North Kids Learning Center
Anderson, IN

Developing X-rays
Literacy Center

For this partner center, give each child black paper programmed with a simple skeleton drawing (minus the rib cage). Place paper squares—each labeled with a letter, most of which are *X*—facedown. For each *X*, provide one cotton swab (left and right rib). A youngster turns over a square. If it shows an *X*, he places the square near his page and adds a rib to the skeleton. If it does not, he leaves the square faceup and his turn is over. Play continues, in turn, until all the cards are flipped. *Recognizing letters*

Karin Bulkow
Washington School for Comprehensive Literacy
Sheboygan, WI

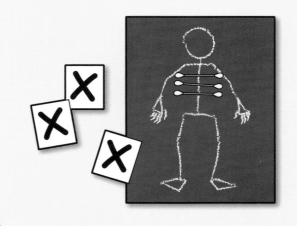

Brush It Off
Writing Center

Write letters on your dry-erase board and then make a card for each letter. Provide several chunky paintbrushes. A child chooses a card and finds the corresponding letter. Then she traces over the letter with a paintbrush. Finally, she uses the paintbrush to completely erase the letter. *Early writing skills*

Nancy Foss
Wee Care Preschool
Galion, OH

Learning Centers

Snowball Letters
Literacy Center

Provide white pom-poms, cotton balls, and crumpled tissue paper. Also provide several large letter cards and sheets of blue (or black) construction paper. A youngster chooses a card and runs his finger over the letter. He identifies the letter, with help as needed. Then he arranges items of his choice on a blank sheet of paper to form the letter. When he is satisfied, he glues the items in place. **For extra fun**, have students drizzle glue on the items and then sprinkle glitter on the glue. *Forming letters, identifying letters*

Penguin Pal Prints
Art Center

Avocados are the key to this printmaking masterpiece! Slice an under-ripe avocado in half and remove the pit. Then place the halves near a shallow pan of black paint. A youngster presses an avocado half into the paint and makes a print on the paper. She makes several more prints in the same way. When the paint is dry, she uses crayons and paper scraps to add feet, beaks, and eyes to the prints to transform them into penguins. *Developing fine-motor skills*

Janet Boyce
Cokato, MN

Stuff It!
Math Center

Provide mittens in different sizes and a variety of manipulatives, such as milk caps, linking cubes, and pom-poms. A child chooses a mitten and a manipulative type. Then he counts as he places manipulatives in the mitten. He repeats the process with a different mitten, noting whether more manipulatives or fewer manipulatives fit compared to the first mitten. **For advanced little ones**, encourage them to estimate the number of items that will fit before placing the items in a mitten. *Counting, comparing sets, estimating*

Mary Ellen Moore, Miller Elementary, Canton, MI

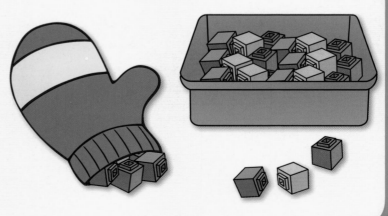

Learning Centers

Mint and Mix
Writing Center

Place cocoa mix in a tray and provide a wrapped candy cane. Encourage youngsters to hold the candy cane by the crook and use it to write in the cocoa mix. **For more advanced youngsters**, provide holiday-related picture-word cards as well! *Forming letters*

Janet Boyce
Cokato, MN

Bird Feeder Fun!
Fine–Motor Area

Get a box of *O*-shaped cereal and place some in a tub. Put the tub at a center with a supply of pipe cleaners. Each little one strings cereal pieces on a pipe cleaner. Then he twists the ends of the pipe cleaner together to make a loop. Each child hangs his pipe cleaner on a low branch of a tree so the birds can nibble on the cereal! *Developing fine-motor skills*

Christine Bausenwein
Early Discoveries Center
Port Jefferson, NY

Ice Cube Slide!
Discovery Center

Attach lengths of PVC pipe together. Then lean the construction against a bookcase or chair. (Use tape to hold it in place if needed.) Place a container of ice cubes at the top of the construction and a tray or tub at the bottom. A child drops an ice cube in the pipe and then waits until it shoots out of the other end, observing to see if it is caught by the tray. (You may wish to place a towel beneath the tray to avoid any wet spots on the floor.) *Observing, exploring motion*

Michelle Gould
Temple Beth Torah
Ventura, CA

Learning Centers

Rainbow Reminder
Snack Center

For each child, place a sampling of each of the following items on a paper plate: strawberry slices (red), cheddar cheese (orange), banana slices (yellow), fresh broccoli (green), blueberries (blue), and grape halves (purple). Name a color and have a child name the corresponding food. Continue with each food option. Then invite little ones to nibble on their rainbow of goodies! *Developing healthy snack habits, identifying colors*

Cynthia Billings
Kay's ABC's of Child Care
Belton, MO

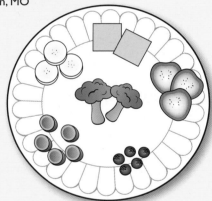

Sheep Shearing
Fine-Motor Area

Glue cotton fiberfill (wool) to a poster board sheep cutout. After the glue dries, put the sheep in your fine-motor area and place scissors and a bag nearby. A youngster uses the scissors to "shear" the sheep's wool; then he places the sheared wool in the bag. Students visit the center until the sheep is sheared and the bag is full of wool. *Fine-motor skills*

Kathy Carson
Dutch Neck Presbyterian Church Cooperative Nursery School
Princeton Junction, NJ

Outside the Box
Literacy Center

Cut apart a copy of the cards on page 81 and gather six small boxes with lids. (Bracelet boxes work great!) Attach one half of each rhyming pair to a different box lid; then place the remaining cards in the boxes, mismatching several of them. A child chooses a box and says the picture word shown on the lid; then she opens the box and says the picture word on the card inside. If the words rhyme, she puts the lid back on the box and sets it aside. If they do not rhyme, she removes the card from the box. At the end, she places all the loose cards in the appropriate boxes. *Rhyming*

Marcell Gibison, Ephrata Church of the Brethren Children's Center, Ephrata, PA

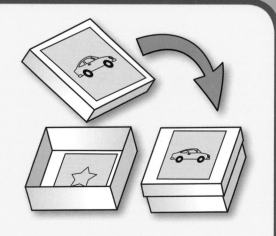

Nifty Hat!
Math Center

Follow up a read-aloud of *The Cat in the Hat* by Dr. Seuss with this fun activity! Set out a large white tagboard top hat, red play dough, and a jumbo die. A child rolls the die and counts the dots. Then she makes that many play dough stripes and places them on the hat. She counts the stripes and the dots to confirm that the amounts are the same; then she removes the stripes and repeats the process. To make the activity **more challenging,** replace the die with number cards.
Counting, making sets

Ilona Spatola
Calico Cat Preschool
South River, NJ

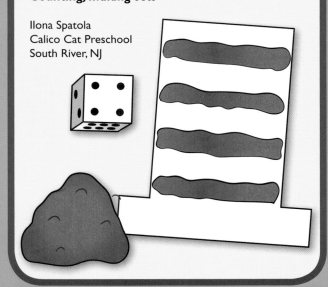

Crystal Clean Choppers
Water Table

Little ones will love this animal dental-care center! Place in your water table plastic animals with visible teeth. Also provide unused toothbrushes and a condiment cup filled with toothpaste. A child dips the bristles of a toothbrush in the toothpaste and then brushes an animal's teeth. When he's finished, he dips the animal in the water and rinses off its pearly whites!
Fine-motor skills

Rebecca Cook
North Phoenix Baptist Preschool
Phoenix, AZ

Presidential Proclamation
Writing Center

In advance, trim an upper-body photo of each child. Give him a sheet of paper programmed with the title "If I Were President!" along with a paper speech bubble and a brown rectangle cutout (podium) programmed as shown. Direct each child to glue the photo, the podium, and the speech bubble to the page as shown; then encourage him to write his name on the podium. Ask, "If you were president, what new rule—or law—would you make?" Record his response on the speech bubble; then invite him to add desired details to the page.
Writing, dictating information

Rebecca Bernard, Children's Creative Learning Center of Framingham
Framingham, MA

If I Were President!

Landon
for President

Learning Centers

Exemplary Egg
Fine-Motor Area

For each child, set out a large craft foam egg cutout with holes punched around the edge. Provide lengths of satin ribbon and self-adhesive craft foam shapes. A child threads a length of ribbon through each hole. When the lacing is complete, an adult helper ties the loose ends of the ribbon into a bow; then the child decorates the egg with desired shapes. *Fine-motor skills*

Mary Gallagher
Edgerton Elementary
Edgerton, OH

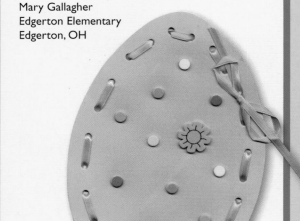

Pom-Pom Painters
Art Center

Attach pom-poms to craft sticks and then place each one next to a shallow pan of paint. A child chooses a stick and presses the pom-pom in the paint. Then she bounces and brushes the pom-pom on her paper. She continues with other pom-pom painters and paint colors. *Expressing oneself with art*

Carole Watkins
Timothy Ball Elementary
Crown Point, IN

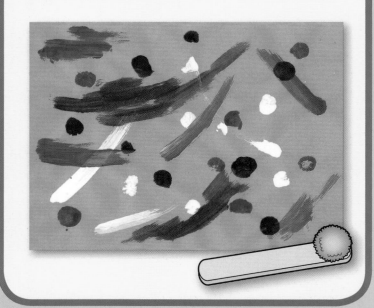

Bye-Bye Birdie
Dramatic-Play Area

Little ones will flock to your dramatic-play area when they see these bird-themed props! Make a supply of bird beaks by attaching craft foam beak cutouts to safety glasses or goggles. Use safety pins (or hot glue) to attach feather boas to the arms of sweatshirts. Also provide lengths of yarn (worms), scarves and fabric scraps (for nest building), and plastic eggs. Youngsters put on the glasses and sweatshirts and take part in bird-themed play! *Pretend play, gross-motor skills*

Amy Brinton, Garden Heights Preschool, Madison, WI

Patriotic Hearts
Literacy Center

Give each youngster a heart cutout from page 82. Provide red paper strips, blue crayons, star stickers, scissors, and glue. Have each child color the top-left section of the heart blue and then decorate it with star stickers. Next, have her glue a paper strip to each shaded area; then help her trim any excess paper from the edge of the heart. (Or, if desired, simply have her color the shaded areas red.) Finally, encourage her to tell what she loves most about the Fourth of July as you record her response on a paper strip. Display the hearts and dictations with the title "We Love the Fourth of July!" *Fine-motor skills, dictating to share information*

Jennifer Davis, Commodore Perry Elementary
Hadley, PA

I love watching fireworks on the Fourth of July!

Beach Blast!
Dramatic-Play Area

Get a blue blanket and a brown blanket (water and beach) and use tape to attach them to the floor in your dramatic-play area. Stock the area with medium-size seashells (or seashell cutouts), plastic pails and shovels, and other beach-related items—like beach towels, sunglasses, a beach ball, and a cooler. Youngsters use the props to engage in pretend beach-related play. *Pretend play*

adapted from an idea by Keely Saunders
Bonney Lake ECEAP
Bonney Lake, WA

Tiny Turtles
Sensory Center

Place two shallow tubs side by side, one filled with water (ocean) and the other with sand (beach). Bury in the sand several plastic eggs, each containing a small toy (or craft foam) turtle. A youngster digs an egg out of the sand and then opens it to help the baby turtle "hatch" from the egg. Then he walks the turtle along the sand to the ocean and swims it around. He continues in the same way until all the turtles are hatched. *Exploring the senses*

Roxanne LaBell Dearman, NC Intervention for the Deaf and Hard of Hearing, Charlotte, NC

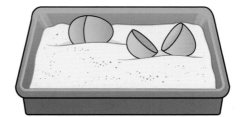

TEC41069

TEC41071

TEC41071

TEC41071

TEC41071

TEC41071

TEC41071

TEC41071

TEC41071

TEC41071

TEC41071

TEC41071

TEC41071

Heart Pattern
Use with "Patriotic Hearts" on page 79.

TEC41073

LITTLE MUSCLES
BIG MUSCLES

Little Muscles BIG Muscles

Pom-Pom Pictures

Provide a bin of pom-poms and simple stencils or die-cuts. A child chooses a stencil and then places pom-poms within the outline. He repeats the process with other stencils. **For a more challenging option,** have little ones use tongs (or a spring-style clothespin) to pick up and place the pom-poms.

Janet Boyce
Cokato, MN

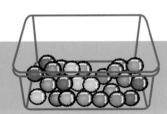

Tennis Ball Toss

Gather tennis balls (or another type of small ball) and place them in a container near a tape line. Put a laundry basket a few feet away from the tape line. Encourage youngsters to sit on the line and attempt to toss the balls into the laundry basket.

Connie Massingill
Dawn 'til Dusk Daycare
Zionsville, IN

Ribbon Dancers

Give each child a length of ribbon (or crepe paper streamer) and have her stand. Then lead youngsters in singing the song several times while they move their ribbons as described.

(sung to the tune of "Alouette")

Ribbon dancers, we are ribbon dancers.
Ribbon dancers, swirling all around.
We can swirl to the left.
We can swirl to the right.
To the left, to the right,
To the left, to the right,
Oh, oh, oh, oh.

Stand and swirl your ribbon.
Swirl your ribbon up high and down low.
Swirl your ribbon to the left.
Swirl your ribbon to the right.
Swirl it to the left and then right.
Swirl it to the left and then right.
Swirl it down to the floor and then up again.

Sarah Booth, Messiah Nursery School, South Williamsport, PA

Sticky-Note Rubbings

Attach sticky notes to a tabletop and provide copy paper and crayons with the wrappers removed. A child places a sheet of paper over the sticky notes. (Lightly tape the paper down if needed.) Then she rubs the side of a crayon over the paper. She moves the paper and repeats the process as many times as desired.

Janet Boyce
Cokato, MN

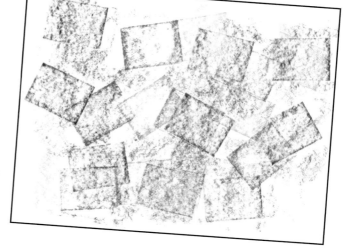

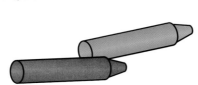

Little Muscles BIG Muscles

Fine motor

Spider's Prey

Provide a spiderweb cutout, plastic insects, tweezers, and a child-size black glove (spider) decorated as desired. A child uses the tweezers to place the insects on the web. Then she dons the spider, crawls it on the web, and "captures" an insect with her pincer grasp (spider fangs). She sets the insect aside and continues until the spider has captured all its prey.

Janet Boyce, Cokato, MN

Gross motor

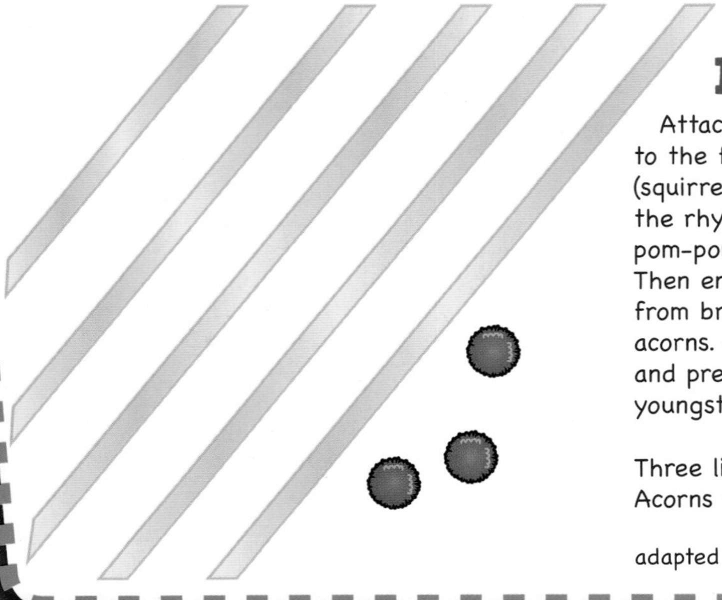

Busy Squirrels

Attach parallel tape lines (branches) to the floor. Encourage three youngsters (squirrels) to stand on the top branch. Say the rhyme shown as you drop three brown pom-poms (acorns) below the bottom branch. Then encourage the three squirrels to jump from branch to branch until they reach the acorns. Prompt each squirrel to take an acorn and pretend to bury it. Continue with other youngsters.

Three little squirrels crawling in a tree,
Acorns fall down—one, two, three!

adapted from an idea by Janet Boyce

Falling Foliage

Suspend a length of twine at students' eye level; then clip spring-style clothespins to the twine. Provide the same number of fall-color leaf cutouts as clothespins. A child clips a leaf to each clothespin. Then she pinches each clothespin to release the leaf and watches it float to the ground. Happy fall!

Janet Boyce, Cokato, MN

Pop, Pop, Pop!

Have youngsters crouch down and pretend to be popcorn kernels in a pan. Then recite the rhyme, demonstrating the actions for children to follow. For added fun, place Bubble Wrap cushioning material on the floor for little ones to stomp on at the end of the rhyme!

Popcorn kernels in a pan,
Laying still as long as they can.
The oil starts to get really hot.
The kernels wiggle in the pot.
They start to cook and hop, hop, hop!
Then all the kernels pop, pop, pop!

Crouch down.
Balance in crouching position.
Rise up slowly and stand.
Wiggle your body.
Hop up and down.
Repeatedly stomp your feet.

Little Muscles BIG Muscles

Fine motor

Miniature Candy Cane Golf

Attach white circle cutouts to a table. (For more thematic fun, decorate them like mint candies!) Attach a plastic milk cap (golf tee) to one end of the table and place a large white pom-pom (snowball) on the tee. Provide a regular-size wrapped candy cane (club). A child uses the candy cane club to hit the snowball and make it land on the circle cutouts.

Janet Boyce, Cokato, MN

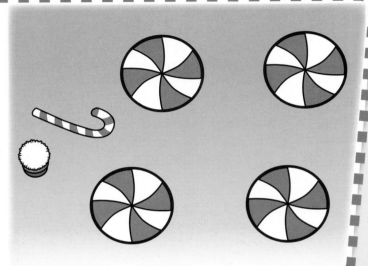

Gross motor

Snowflake Groove

Give each child a paper doily snowflake and then lead the group in performing this cute action rhyme. For added fun, put on a favorite seasonal recording when the rhyme ends and encourage little ones to do their best snowflake groove!

Drift to the left,	*Float snowflake to the left.*
Drift to the right,	*Float snowflake to the right.*
Float to the ground,	*Float snowflake to the ground.*
And melt out of sight.	*Hold snowflake behind your back.*
Snowflakes move	*Float snowflake in the air.*
Gently past your face,	*Float snowflake past your face.*
Twirling around	*Twirl snowflake around.*
With snowy grace.	
This is the way	*Float snowflake in the air.*
That snowflakes move.	
Now it's time to do	
The snowflake groove!	*Dance around with snowflake.*

Tricia Kylene Brown, Bowling Green, KY

Hanging Icicles

Mold a supply of "icicles" from aluminum foil, being sure to flatten the top of each icicle for easy bending. Suspend a length of clothesline or twine in a traffic-free area. A child bends the top of each icicle over the line and squeezes it to hook it in place. (Or provide spring-style clothespins and have youngsters clip the icicles to the line.) What a lovely line of glistening icicles!

Janet Boyce, Cokato, MN

Seasonal Corners

Invite youngsters to play this fun adaptation of Four Corners. Post in each corner of the room a seasonal cutout, such as a Christmas tree, a dreidel, a snowman, and an ornament. For each cutout, place an identical shape in a bag. Hand the bag to a volunteer; then prompt each classmate to stand in a corner of his choosing. When everyone is in place, have the volunteer take a shape from the bag, call out the shape name, and then put the shape back in the bag. Instruct each child standing in the designated corner to march, hop, tiptoe, or crawl to the group-time area and sit down. Standing youngsters can then choose a new corner in which to stand if desired. Then the child pulls a cutout from the bag and students repeat the process. Play continues until everyone is seated.

Dianne Giggey
Episcopal Day School
Pensacola, FL

Little Muscles BIG Muscles

Toothy Patterns

Cut wavy-edged bulletin board border into small sections so they resemble teeth. Then place the teeth at a table along with an open mouth cutout as shown. Youngsters arrange the teeth in the mouth to create fun patterns. What gorgeous teeth!

Janet Boyce
Cokato, MN

These also make fun individual projects! Simply have youngsters glue the teeth in place!

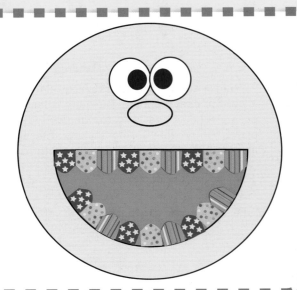

Hurry Scurry!

Make a class supply of circle cutouts (burrows), minus one. Place a sticker on the back of one burrow. Then scatter the burrows around an open area, with the sticker-side down on that burrow. Choose a volunteer. Then have each remaining child stand on a burrow. Have the volunteer say, "Groundhogs, groundhogs, find a new burrow!" Have each child scurry like a groundhog to stand on a different burrow. Then prompt each child to check the bottom of his burrow. The child with the sticker becomes the new caller. Rearrange the burrows to hide the sticker. Then play another round.

Lauren Beneke
Atonement Children's Weekday Ministries
Fargo, ND

Chock-full o' Chocolates!

Place candy cup paper liners in an empty candy box. Provide brown pom-poms (chocolate candy) and a pair of tongs. A child uses the tongs to place a piece of chocolate in each candy cup. She continues until the box is chock-full of chocolates.

Janet Boyce, Cokato, MN

Clean Your Rooms!

Divide the class into two groups and have each group stand on opposite sides of the room. For each group, scatter the same number of soft items—such as stuffed animals, pillows, balls, and dress-up clothes—onto the floor. Provide each team with an empty container. Set a timer and call out, "Clean your rooms!" Then encourage each team to clean its "room" as quickly as possible. When time runs out, prompt everyone to stop cleaning. Then count the items in each container to determine which team has the cleanest room. What a great rainy day activity!

Leigh-Ann Jacob
Christ Church Preschool
Oxford, CT

Little Muscles BIG Muscles

Bunny Brunch

Set out a stuffed toy rabbit, a food dish, and a supply of orange and green paper scraps (carrots and lettuce). A child tears the carrots and lettuce into bite-size pieces, dropping them in the food dish for the bunny to "eat." For a follow-up activity, invite her to glue a bunny cutout to construction paper and then glue the carrots and lettuce around the bunny.

Janet Boyce, Cokato, MN

Hoppin' Along

Attach a row of colorful lily pad cutouts on your floor. Have several youngsters (frogs) line up near one end of the lily pads and the remaining children sit on a nearby "log." Frogs, in turn, jump from lily pad to lily pad, saying the names of the colors as they go. If a frog gets stuck, the youngsters on the log help him out! When finished, he sits on the log.

Trisha Kuiper
The Learning Tree Preschool
Omaha, NE

Munch, Munch!

Attach a row of green pom-poms (caterpillar) to a hole puncher as shown. (Hint: E6000 adhesive—for adult use only—will glue just about anything to anything else.) Provide leaf cutouts. A child pretends the hungry caterpillar is munching a tasty leaf as he punches holes around the edges.

Janet Boyce, Cokato, MN

Beanbag Boogie

Gather several beanbags and a bucket. Arrange youngsters so they're standing in a circle and place the bucket in the middle. Hand a child a beanbag and have students pass it around the circle as you say the chant shown. At the end of the chant, prompt the child holding the beanbag to toss it in the bucket. If the beanbag lands in the bucket, little ones dance around and chant "Beanbag boogie!" If not, hand the next child a beanbag and continue the game until all the beanbags have been used.

Pass the beanbag hand to hand.
When it's tossed, where will it land?

Marie E. Cecchini, West Dundee, IL

Little Muscles BIG Muscles

Fine motor

Veggie Kabobs

Provide a makeshift barbecue grill, unsharpened pencils or thin dowel pieces (skewers), large stringing beads (vegetable chunks), and a tray. If desired, provide an apron for added fun. A child slides several vegetables onto each skewer to make veggie kabobs. When she's finished, she "grills" the kabobs and then places them on the tray.

Janet Boyce, Cokato, MN

Gross motor

Feeding Frenzy

Hold one end of a blue blanket or sheet and have an adult volunteer hold the other end. Have students stand next to the blanket and pretend to be sandpipers (a type of bird that pokes its bill into the sand to feed on insects). After a few moments, wiggle the blanket up and down to mimic a rippling wave coming in to shore. This will prompt your sandpipers to run away before the wave gets them. When the wave calms and retreats, have your little birds come back to their former positions and resume their foraging activities. Repeat this shoreline feeding frenzy for several rounds.

Jana Sanderson, Rainbow School, Stockton, CA

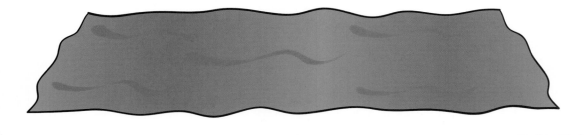

Ice Cold!

Provide a small cooler with white or blue cube blocks (or craft foam squares). Also provide several plastic cups and tongs. A child uses the tongs to remove the blocks (ice cubes) from the cooler and place them in the cups. When he's finished he pretends to drink up the icy beverages.

Janet Boyce, Cokato, MN

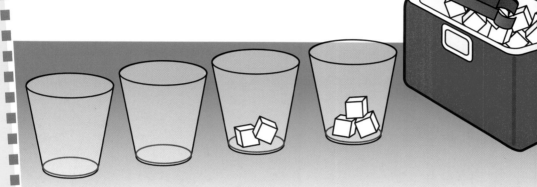

Imitation Popcorn

Seat all but one student in a circle. Give the standing child several yellow pom-poms (popcorn kernels). Have him walk around the inside of the circle and drop each kernel in a different child's lap as you lead the group in saying the chant shown. Then have the chosen children go to the middle of the circle and jump up and down, pretending to be popcorn kernels popping in a pot. Repeat the activity until each child has had a turn to be a popcorn kernel.

Popcorn kernels pop, pop, pop.
Get them ready for the pot!

Laura Kessler, Stoneridge Elementary, Roseville, CA

Super Sunflower!

©The Mailbox® • TEC41068 • Aug./Sept. 2013

Note to the teacher: Give each child a copy of this page and have her color it as desired. Next, have her dip a finger in brown paint and then make fingerprints (seeds) in the middle of the sunflower.

A Firefighter's Friend

©The Mailbox® • TEC41069 • Oct./Nov. 2013

Note to the teacher: Give each child a copy of this page. Encourage him to use a red crayon to trace and color the firefighter hat and fire hydrant. Then have him press his fingertip on a black ink pad and on the dog to make spots so the dog resembles a dalmatian.

Stringing the Lights

Note to the teacher: Give each child a copy of this page and encourage her to trace the lines. Then have her make colorful fingerprints along the lines so they resemble strings of holiday lights.

Peep, Peep, Peep!

©The Mailbox® • TEC41072 • April/May 2014

Note to the teacher: Give a child a copy of the page. Then have him dip a pencil eraser in yellow paint and make prints (grain) along the lines for the chicks to follow to get to their mothers.

Picnic Time!

©The Mailbox® • TEC41073 • June/July 2014

Note to the teacher: Have each child color a copy of this page. Encourage her to press her fingertip on a black ink pad and then on each blank space on the blanket to make fingerprint ants. Have her use a fine-tip black marker to add details to each ant.

Management Tips & Timesavers

Management Tips & Timesavers

Pick a Song

Display a large tree cutout. Program apple cutouts with different song titles and drawings. Use removable adhesive to attach the apples to the tree. Each day, invite a child to pick a song from the tree. Then lead the group in singing the song. *Abby Boruff, Clive Elementary, Windsor Heights, IA*

Work Space

To keep work materials organized, use Con-Tact covering to attach a seasonal nametag to each child's work space. During projects, the student places his crayons and glue on his nametag; during snacktime, this is where his milk or juice will sit. It's an easy way to get organized and reduce spills! *Claudine Fredy, Iola-Scandinavia Elementary, Iola, WI*

Take a Turn

Remind youngsters to take turns with this toe-tapping ditty. *Suzanne Moore, Tucson, AZ*

(sung to the tune of "The Wheels on the Bus")

[We all work together taking turns],
Taking turns, taking turns.
[We all work together taking turns]
All through the day.

Continue with the following: *We'll all play together taking turns; You take your turn, and I'll take mine*

Nifty Names

Personalize a card for each child and then attach a different sticker to each card. Set out the cards each morning. When a child arrives, he finds his card and places it in a pocket chart. Afterward, hold up each card and encourage that child to stand. After a few weeks of practice, begin placing your hand over the sticker so a youngster has to identify his card based only on his name. *Ann Miller, Ann's Bright Beginnings Preschool, Paulding, OH*

Quick Notes

Here's an easy way to keep a record of small behavior problems. For each child, label an index card and place the cards in a file box. When a problem occurs, jot a brief note about what happened and how it was resolved. If you need to speak with a child's parent about her behavior, you can quickly refer to your notes. *Mary Gilchrist, YMCA Preschool, Washington, IA*

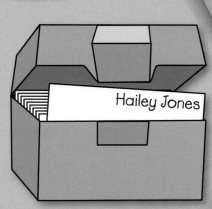

Management Tips & Timesavers

Seasonal Binders

Looking for a way to minimize the amount of storage space needed for theme materials? Divide three-ring binders into sections for each theme, using one binder per season. Then, for each theme, put materials such as lesson plans, reproducibles, songs, and photos of related crafts and displays in plastic page protectors. Store the page protectors in the binder behind the correct divider. *Teresa Ellingen, Risen Savior Preschool, Ft. Wayne, IN*

Fall

Watching a Movie

Here's a quick and easy way to help youngsters settle down at naptime. Have students lie down and close their eyes. Begin playing an audio book and tell students to pretend they are watching a movie, picturing what is happening in their minds. *Melody Gann, Creative World, Apollo Beach, FL*

Make a Line

This simple and magical phrase helps little ones stand and walk in a line! Have a child get in line. Then, for each remaining child, say "Get behind the last person." This phrase is easily understood, and soon your little ones will be pros! *Janice Sutherland, Louisiana Schnell Elementary, Placerville, CA*

Squeaky Clean

To get students in the habit of always using soap when they wash their hands, sniff each child's hands after he washes them. If you smell soap, say, "Super squeaky clean!" Eventually everyone's hands will be squeaky clean the first time. *Beth Sharpe, The Malvern School of Medford, Medford, NJ*

Staying Together

Keeping books and matching CDs together is a snap! Put the CD in a CD envelope. Place the envelope on the inside back cover of the book. Then use clear packing tape to attach the envelope to the cover, being sure to leave one side open so the CD can be removed. *Kathleen Bergman, Quad Care, Lomira, WI*

Hand Soap

Management Tips & Timesavers

A Note of Thanks

Print copies of a class photo. When you need a thank-you card, glue a class photo to a construction paper card and write "Thank You!" above it. On the inside of the card, write a message and then help each child sign it. *Mary Ann Craven, Fallbrook United Methodist Preschool, Fallbrook, CA*

Lineup and Classroom Jobs

Attach large sequential number cards to the floor where students line up. Assign a classroom job to each number. Line up students, making sure that each child is on a different number. During that week, each child lines up on his number and is responsible for the job assigned to that number. The next week, the child who stood on "1" moves to the last number and everyone else moves up one. *Leslie Hage, St. Vincent's Academy, Orlando, FL*

Who's Listening?

To capture your youngsters' attention, sing the song shown using an owl pointer (a craft stick with an owl cutout) to point to the named body part. Substitute body parts as needed. *Debbie Bartsch, Gloria Dei Preschool, Crestview Hills, KY*

(sung to the tune of "Where Is Thumbkin?")

Who is listening?
Who is listening?
Touch your [nose].
Touch your [nose].
If you are listening,
If you are listening,
Touch your [nose].
Touch your [nose].

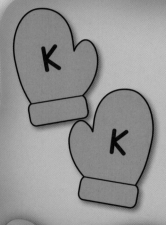

Mitten Match Transition

For each child, label a pair of mitten cutouts with matching letters. Separate the pairs to make two sets. When youngsters have to wait for their turns, distribute one set of mittens. Hold up a mitten from the other set. The child with the matching mitten brings it to you and then takes his turn. *Audrey Kelly, Half Pints Learning Center, Tewksbury, MA*

Positive Behavior Trees

Post a personalized tree cutout for each child. Whenever a youngster demonstrates good behavior, invite him to put an ornament (sticky dot) on his tree. After he earns a given number of ornaments, give him a star sticker to put at the top of his tree and have him take his tree home. *Jennifer Gelfman, Ohio Valley Voices, Cincinnati, OH*

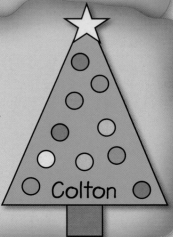

Management Tips & Timesavers

Yarn Holders

When you finish a pack of moist wipes, don't throw the container away! Reuse it for yarn! Simply wash and dry the container. Then pop the ball of yarn in the container and feed it out through the top. Now it's simple for youngsters to cut lengths of yarn for arts-and-crafts projects. *Talin T. Sant, Early Childhood Center of Paterson 1, Paterson, NJ*

No More Messy Puzzles!

Here's a handy puzzle-storing tip! When you store puzzles in your theme bins, wrap them with Glad Press'n Seal wrap to keep the pieces in place. No more hunting around the bin for missing pieces! *Stefanie Washinger, Ready to Learn Preschool at Gideon Pond Elementary, Burnsville, MN*

Supersize Song Cards

Print words to popular songs and fingerplays with coordinating clip art and then attach the printout to a file folder. Store the file folders in your reading area. This makes them handy to grab when needed during circle time, and children will love "reading" them during center time. *Amy Lange, All God's Children Preschool, Delafied, WI*

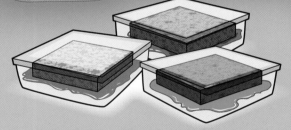

Stamp Pads in All Colors

Place a sponge in each of several sandwich-size plastic containers. Saturate each sponge with a different color of paint and then attach the lid. Now you have many colors of oversize stamp pads that can be used for printing with vegetables, spools, stampers, and other items. Simply add more paint as needed. *Martha Whitaker, Loving Start Preschool, Milwaukee, WI*

Three Minutes!

To help your preschoolers with sharing issues, implement this strategy! When a child wants a turn with a toy, instruct him to ask, "May I please have a turn?" Then direct the child with the toy to say, "Yes, in three minutes." Keep track of the time and prompt the child to pass the toy on after three minutes. This consistently applied rule gives both youngsters a degree of control and stops many sharing squabbles! *Carol Warren, Valley View Baptist Church, Tuscaloosa, AL*

Management Tips & Timesavers

Match the Dots

Help little ones put their shoes on the correct foot every time with this tip. Draw two small dots on a pair of shoes as shown. Before a child puts his shoes on, he sets them side by side, making sure that the dots are "looking" at each other. Then he puts his shoes on! *Marjie Koons, Marjie's Christian Daycare, Lansing, MI*

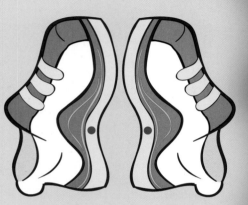

Stop and Go

This fun tip encourages youngsters to pay attention while walking in a line. When you need students to stop, say, "Red light." When you are ready for students to resume moving, say, "Green light." *Caroline Warkentin, Lil Champions, Williams Lake, WA*

Super Circle Sitters

To encourage listening skills, write "Super Circle Sitter" on each of two foam visors and then use stickers or foam shapes to decorate them. During a circle-time activity, quietly place the visors on the heads of two children who are exhibiting exceptional listening skills! *Elizabeth Munson, Kennett Square Head Start, Kennett Square, PA*

Kindness Toss

Promote kindness in your classroom! Label a plastic pail as shown. Then place the pail in the center of your circle. Invite each child to name a way that he will show kindness that day and then "toss" it in the pail. Return the pail to its place, being sure to make a show of how heavy the pail is when it is full of kindness. *Ellen Maguire, Little Corner School House, Brookline, MA*

Magazine Saver

Have some of the pages come out of the binding of your well-loved issues of *The Mailbox* magazine? Here's the solution to your problem. Take your magazines to an office supply store. They will cut off the original binding and attach a spiral binding. It's inexpensive, and the magazine pages lay flat! *Nancy Guyot, Hadnot Point Child Development Center, Hadnot Point, NC*

Our Readers Share

Our Readers SHARE

First Aid Fun

When I put out my medical prop box for dramatic play, my little ones are always eager to "fix" broken bones. So I came up with these simple cast props! I cut off the toes and elastic tops of white adult socks. My youngsters can just slip the socks onto their legs or arms to pretend they're wearing casts. *Twilla Lamm, Little Dixie Head Start, Hugo, OK*

POSITIVELY PROUD PARENTS

I boost youngsters' self-esteem with this idea. Once a month, I assign "parent homework." I send home programmed seasonal clip art. (See the box for a list of clip art and programming suggestions.) A parent completes the note and returns it to school. I read the note to the class and then add it to a display titled "Positively Proud Parents." At the end of the school year, I use each child's notes to make a special booklet for him. *Linda Aguiar, Learning Lane, Taunton, MA*

_____ is the apple of my eye because

I am nuts about _____ because

September (apple)	_____ is the apple of my eye because
October (acorn)	I am nuts about _____ because
November (turkey)	I am thankful for _____ because
December (gift)	_____ is a gift because
January (star)	_____ is a star because
February (heart)	I honestly love _____ because
March (shamrock)	I am lucky to have _____ because
April (umbrella)	_____ showers me with happiness when
May (flower)	_____ is blooming in so many ways because
June (sun)	_____ brightens my life because

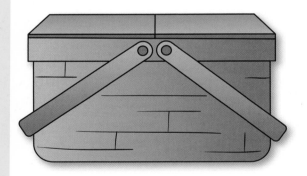

The MAILBOX BLOG

Picnic in the Park

Prior to the beginning of the new school year, I invite each family to join me at a local park for a picnic. Families bring their own lunches, and I provide cookies for dessert. I have found that this get-together eases youngsters' worries about the first day of school! *Darlene Butler Taig, Willow Creek Cooperative Preschool, Westland, MI*

BOTTLE CAP OPTIONS!

Bottle caps are inexpensive manipulatives that can be used in a variety of ways. For each child, I program caps with the letters of her name and place them in a resealable plastic bag. Then she can practice arranging caps to spell her name. I also label caps with numbers for youngsters to practice number recognition and number order.

Annette Warren, First Baptist Child Development Center, Taylorsville, NC

The MAILBOX BLOG

Designer Mats

For each child, I laminate a personalized sheet of construction paper. Then I use the resulting mats for seating in our group area. At the end of circle time each day, I give each child a theme-related sticker to attach to his mat. By the end of the school year, the mats look lovely and reflect the themes we've studied!

Darlene Butler Taig, Willow Creek Cooperative Preschool, Westland, MI

Daily Practice

Combine vocabulary practice with the task of taking attendance. Prior to taking attendance each day, I name a category such as animals, toys, or food. In turn, I call each child's name, and the child responds with the name of something that belongs in that category. *Jo Carol Hebert, ABC Dual Language Learning Center, Bryan, TX*

Unique Notes

To make colorful thank-you postcards for parents and visitors, I place sheets of poster board, paint, and paintbrushes in my art area. I invite my youngsters to paint designs on the poster board. When the paint is dry, I cut the poster boards into postcards. So simple! **Carole Watkins, Timothy Ball Elementary, Crown Point, IN**

The MAILBOX BLOG

Quiet Spray

I remind little ones when it's quiet time with "quiet spray"! I make a label that says "Quiet Spray" and attach it to an empty spray bottle. Anytime I need my youngsters to be quiet, I "spray" this magical spray around them. Just a few sprays is all it takes! *Stacie Clements, Florida Mesa Preschool and Childcare Center, Durango, CO*

Our Readers SHARE

TRICK OR TREAT

Each year, my school does this safe yet fun alternative to neighborhood trick-or-treating. In advance, we ask parents to donate wrapped candy. On or near Halloween, volunteers station themselves behind closed doors at the school. Then parents walk little ones from door to door to trick-or-treat! *Mary Ann Craven, Fallbrook United Methodist Preschool, Fallbrook, CA*

Planting Pumpkins

Looking for a way to use all those pumpkin seeds that are left after you carve a pumpkin? Try this! I help each child plant a few seeds in a personalized cup. Then I encourage her to water her seeds often. After the seeds begin to grow into plants, I send each child's plant home with her. My youngsters love watching their pumpkin plants grow. *Analisa Lopez, Ascension Lutheran Preschool, Rolling Hills Estates, CA*

Point It Out!

When I assign jobs to my youngsters each week, I give one child the job of being the chart pointer. This helper uses a special pointer to point to the letter of the day. I may also ask him to point to the letter his name begins with, letters that make a certain sound, or a letter that I name. This is a fun job for my students, and it's a quick way for me to do a bit of assessment! *Deborah Eassa, St. Ann's School, Syracuse, NY*

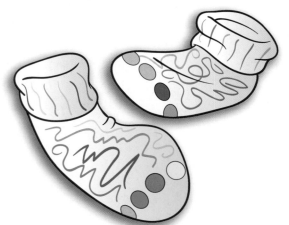

The MAILBOX BLOG

A Wild Day

As an alternative to a Halloween celebration, I have a Wild Thing Day! Youngsters wear their pajamas to school and provide a pair of old socks. They make Wild Thing masks and then decorate their socks with markers and sticky dots (toenails) to make Wild Thing feet! They don their masks and feet, and we have a wild rumpus! My youngsters always have lots of fun with this celebration. *Darlene Butler Taig, Willow Creek Cooperative Preschool, Westland, MI*

Our Readers SHARE

Shake It!

Make paper plate shakers without the worry of the beans or pasta falling out! Place beans or pasta in an envelope and seal it. Then place the envelope between the two decorated paper plates and staple them together. Encourage youngsters to shake these supersafe shakers! *Dee Mulranen, St. James Preschool, Aston, PA*

A "Gourd-geous" Display

During November, I provide a wicker cornucopia, gourds, and fake fall leaves. A child examines the gourds, noticing each one's unique shape and texture. Then she chooses her favorite gourds and leaves and places them in and around the cornucopia to make an eye-catching display. *Donna Ream, Ms. Donna's Daycare, Plainfield, IL*

A Snazzy Scarecrow

To make an in-class scarecrow, I have youngsters tear and crumple newspaper and then stuff the paper into a pair of jeans and a button-down shirt. I put raffia in the ends of the pant legs and the shirt sleeves and use rubber bands to keep it in place. I put a wooden stick down the back of the shirt so the scarecrow will stay seated and then use binder clips to attach the shirt to the pants. Next, I add a milk jug decorated to look like a head and a hat! *Jennifer Schear, Wright Elementary, Cedar Rapids, IA*

Ready to Walk

Our school has a zero-noise policy for the halls. To get my youngsters ready, I lead them in performing the chant shown. *Edna Stivers, Bourbon Central Elementary, Paris, KY*

Every line has a leader	Hold up one finger.
And a caboose.	Hold up two fingers.
Keep your line straight	Stand up straight.
And not too loose.	Wiggle.
Walk and walk	Walk in place.
And walk in a line	
With your hands to yourself.	Put hands by your side.
You'll be just fine.	

(Snap, snap, snap.)

THANKFUL TURKEYS

Prior to Thanksgiving Day, I send home a paper plate with each child. With her family's help, the child decorates the turkey, incorporating things that she is thankful for into the decorations. This is a great family activity, and the turkeys turn out to be very creative! *Sr. Joseph Margaret, Mount Aviat Academy, Childs, MD*

TREE TRIMMING

This holiday craft is a favorite of my students. I cut branches from an old artificial Christmas tree. Then I pour plaster of paris into a clean laundry detergent cap and stick the end of the branch in the plaster. After the plaster hardens, I invite my little ones to decorate the trees. They wrap yarn around the trees so it looks like garlands. Then they use decorative paper punches, scrap paper, and glitter to make ornaments and a star. **Lisa Michael, MCESC Special Needs Preschool, Celina, OH**

A Gift of Love

Here's a sweet gift parents are sure to treasure. I give each child a lidded box and have him pantomime putting a lot of love in the box before putting on the lid. I help him wrap the box. Then I have him attach a bow and a copy of the poem shown. **Connie Burgess, Riverdale Elementary, Courtland, VA**

This gift is very light,
As you can surely see.
But it is filled with something
That comes from little me.
I filled this box with love
And then attached this rhyme—
A very special gift to you
This merry Christmastime!

Ready to Eat!

I begin snacktime (or lunch) by leading youngsters in reciting this adorable rhyme.

We say *please* and *thank you* because it is polite.
We always wait for others before we take a bite.
We love our bread. We love our butter.
But most of all, we love each other!

Eileen Gingras, The Children's School at Deerfield Academy, Deerfield, MA

Paper Plate Comprehension

To review the events of a story, I take photos of the illustrations that show specific events. Then I print the photos and attach them to a paper plate. I also make a set of numbered clothespins. After a read-aloud of the story, I display the paper plate. I invite volunteers to clip the clothespins to the plate to show the order of the story events. *Patti Ferrick, Child Advocates of Blair County—Head Start, Altoona, PA*

Calendar Counting

I cut apart old calendars and laminate the pages. To practice counting, I give each child a calendar page and have him place a small counter on each numbered square as he counts. To review numbers that we have learned, I call out a number and direct him to place a counter in the box with that number. Students can also write each number in its box. *Donna Puchino, Woodside Christian Preschool, Yardley, PA*

★ ★ ★ January ★ ★ ★

S	M	T	W	T	F	S
	1	2	3	4	5	6
7	8	9	10	11	12	13
14	15	16	17	18	19	20
21	22	23	24	25	26	27
28	29	30	31			

Grin and Share It!

During show-and-tell, one of my little boys was sharing a story about a toy he had received. He proudly stated, "I got it from the man who snuck into my house." I had to chuckle after I questioned him about this nighttime intruder to realize he was talking about Santa. *Sue Lein, St. Jude the Apostle, Wauwatosa, WI*

The MAILBOX BLOG

Penguin Pals

For my penguin unit, I have each child lie on a length of white bulletin board paper and then I trace her outline. She colors her outline so she looks like a penguin. Then we cut out the penguins and display them in the hallway! They always look so cute!
Cindy Macdonald, Twice as Nice FCC & Preschool, Raynham, MA

LETTERS TO SANTA

During the holiday season, I have each child dictate a letter to Santa. Then I put the letter in an envelope addressed to Santa and seal it. I attach a copy of the poem shown to the letter and send it home with the child. *Kim Martin, Young Tracks Preschool, Steamboat Springs, CO*

I wrote this letter to Santa
With everything I have to say:
What I wish and want
On this Christmas Day.

There are two options for my letter.
You should decide what you want to do.
You can mail this letter to Santa.
The address is there for you.

Or you can keep this letter
And put it away with care.
Then, when I am big and tall,
We'll have a memory to share.

Lucy Jones
123 Main St.
Greensboro, NC 27410

Santa Claus
North Pole

Our Readers Share

Shadow Search

To prepare for this entertaining Groundhog Day activity, I cut groundhog shadows from black craft foam. While my little ones are out of the room, I hide the shadows. When they return, I invite them to find the shadows. After all the shadows are found, we count them together. *Beth Joyce, Bakerstown Presbyterian Children's Center, Gibsonia, PA*

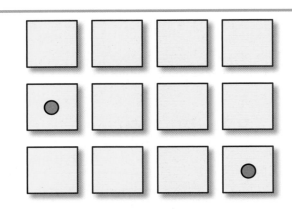

Sticky Ideas

I love sticky dots! Here are just a few of the many ways I use them in my classroom.
- I attach sticky dots to cards to make a game that reinforces color matching.
- I put sticky dots in the writing center. Students use them as pretend postage stamps.
- I program sheets of sticky dots with uppercase and lowercase letters. A child places the dots on a sheet of paper in matching pairs.
- I put sticky dots at the art center. Students use them to make critters, such as caterpillars.

Lizabeth Toby, Newburgh Early Childhood Center, Newburgh, ME

Grin and Share It!

One busy day in preschool, I was feeling a bit overwhelmed with special activities I had planned for the class. Suddenly, two little arms wrapped around my neck and a small voice said, "You sure happier up my day!" That hug and message was a reminder to me that special activities are worth every ounce of effort they take. *Therese M. Durhman, Mountain View Elementary, Hickory, NC*

You sure happier up my day!

From head to toe, I love you so!

A Valentine Keepsake

Parents are sure to love these adorable valentines! I cut and fold valentine-themed scrapbooking paper to make a card for each child. Then I program each card with the message shown. Next, I paint each child's feet and help him make footprints on a card. After the paint is dry, I invite each child to dictate a message to his family on the inside of the card. *Jennifer Williams, Monee Elementary, Monee, IL*

Exchanging Valentines

As a fun alternative to swapping cards for Valentine's Day, I prepare a list of each child's personal interests. I place the lists in a bag and have each child take one. I attach the list to a note asking the child's family to use the list to pick out a book for his classmate. On the day of our Valentine's Day celebration, each child brings the book and gives it to the classmate. *Frani Audet, Westbrook Regional Vocational Center, Westbrook, ME*

Silly Sounds

I fill calendar time with laughter by altering our days of the week song. We sing it our regular way, and then we choose a sound that represents the month, such as an owl's hoot for October or a kissing noise for February. Then the children "sing" the song, replacing all the lyrics with that noise! *Darlene Butler Taig, Willow Creek Cooperative Preschool, Westland, MI*

Shamrock Buddies

I puzzle-cut a shamrock in half for every two students. Each morning during March, a child chooses a shamrock half and then finds her shamrock buddy. She and her shamrock buddy sit, play, and work together for the day. *Cathy Welwood, Learning Experience, Calgary, Alberta, Canada*

Happy 100th Day

In preparation for our 100th Day celebration, I have my youngsters help me create a banner. On a bedsheet, I write a message such as "100 Days Smarter!" or "It's Our 100th Day!" Then I have my students use number stamps to stamp "100" around the message. On the 100th day, we proudly display our banner. *Marlana Pastula, First Steps for Kids, Totowa, NJ*

Familiar Figures

To reenergize my centers, I stock them with items that are sure to capture youngsters' attention. For example, I place magnifying glasses and figures of well-known characters in my science center. I also put familiar character stickers in the writing center. These familiar images also promote conversations between youngsters! *Kate Ensell, Annehurst Elementary, Westerville, OH*

Our Readers Share

Pint-Size Puzzles

To make these easy mini puzzles, I laminate two identical sheets from a decorative notepad. I cut one sheet into a desired number of puzzle pieces and use the other sheet as a puzzle base. Then I store the base and puzzle pieces in a resealable plastic bag. Given the number of pages per pad, I often make personal puzzles for each child to take home and share with her family! *Sandra K. Ten Hagen, CDS Lakeshore Head Start, Zeeland, MI*

On a Roll

Here's an engaging idea that helps build vocabulary! I hang a roll of adding machine paper near my literacy center. Then I help my little ones randomly choose a word from a children's picture dictionary. After discussing the word, I write it on the roll; then, as youngsters choose additional words, each one is written above the previous word. As the list grows, I roll the loose end of the paper and secure it with a paper clip. When I want to review the list with youngsters, I simply unroll the paper. *Kim Love, Territorial Elementary, Chino Valley, AZ*

Elegant Eyewear

To help students who are new to wearing glasses feel more comfortable, I invite everyone to make a special pair of glasses. For each student, I cut off two rings from a plastic soda bottle connector. I have youngsters decorate the rings with materials like glitter glue or tiny stickers. Then I help each child connect two pipe cleaner earpieces to complete the frames. Finally, I read *Arthur's Eyes* by Marc Brown and take a class photo of everyone modeling their eyewear! *Suzanne Foote, East Ithaca Preschool, Ithaca, NY*

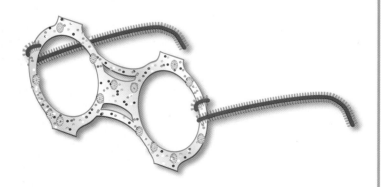

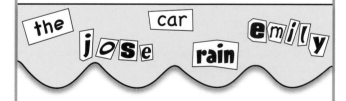

Handmade Border

During our Earth Day celebration, my preschoolers turn old newspapers and magazines into unique classroom decor. I have students cut out large individual words and glue them to plain bulletin board border strips. As they work, we practice letter and word identification. For added fun, I have youngsters cut out individual letters to spell their names. Then we glue the names among the text in the border and play I Spy! *Carole Watkins, Timothy Ball Elementary, Crown Point, IN*

PROBLEM SOLVED!

Problem Solved!

Your Solutions to Classroom Challenges

We **pretend to be mice** following a narrow path through Farmer Fred's garden. As we "scurry" along, I silently prompt my little mice to move as quietly as can be so they don't wake the farmer!

Annie Quinn, Cornerstone Christian Academy, Shelbyville, KY

How do you encourage little ones to *walk in a straight line*?

I hang a **handprint banner** along the wall. As students line up, I have each child touch the handprint nearest him. This helps youngsters form a nice straight line, and then we're ready to move on.

Cynthia Zimmerman, Downingtown, PA

> We cannot hold a torch to light another's path without brightening our own.
> —Ben Sweetland

I lead youngsters in a silent adaptation of **Simon Says**. For example, I walk with my hands on my head, and students do the same. Then I change the movement, and children follow suit. The visual cues help keep little ones alert and focused.

Cortney Nornhold, Abide in the Vine Child Care Center, Owego, NY

To help youngsters form a straight line, I call out, "**Spaghetti!**" prompting them to line up like a giant length of uncooked spaghetti. I repeat the prompt, as needed, to remind students to walk in a straight line.

Nicole Marshall, Nicole's Preschool, Pilot Butte, AL

Spaghetti!

Problem Solved!

Your Solutions to Classroom Challenges

How do you help youngsters with their *scissors skills*?

The art center is a great place for youngsters to practice their cutting skills! On large sheets of paper, I draw zigzag lines. I place the papers and scissors at the art center. A center visitor clips a sheet of paper to the easel and then cuts along the lines.

Christina Kasler, A Home Away From Home Childcare, Vacaville, CA

I make a simple chart, like the one shown, that helps youngsters remember items that are okay to cut, such as paper, and not okay to cut, such as hair. I display the poster at a center and then stock it with items to be cut and various types of scissors.

Sami Pollard, The Children's Place, Decatur, TX

The expert at anything was once a beginner.
—Helen Hayes

I use this simple poem to remind students that holding their scissors correctly will improve their cutting skills.

> Thumb in the thumb hole,
> Fingers all together,
> Point your thumb up to the sky.
> Your cutting will get better.

Marcell Gibison, Ephrata Church of the Brethren Children's Center, Ephrata, PA

Use smiley faces to help your students hold their scissors correctly. Draw a smiley face on each child's pair of scissors in the location shown. When you see a child holding his scissors incorrectly, simply say, "Eyes to the sky." Then he alters the orientation of the scissors so the smiley face is facing up.

Nancy Foss, Wee Care, Galion, OH
Sheryl Keseian, Avon Nursery School, Avon, MA

Problem Solved!

How do you encourage *good personal hygiene* in your classroom?

Your Solutions to Classroom Challenges

 I help youngsters practice blowing air through their noses to help develop **nose-blowing skills**. I encourage little ones to pretend they are big bad wolves trying to blow down the pigs' houses of straw, sticks, and bricks!

Karen Smith, Little Tid-Bits, Fresno, CA

 I take a photo of a child **washing his hands**, making sure to snap a picture for each step. Then I print the photos, label them, and post a set near each student sink. I also print a set of photos for youngsters to use in a sequencing activity.

Martha Cymbaluk, Child-Parent Centers, Tucson, AZ

Washing hands is the best way to reduce the number of germs on them. Alcohol-based sanitizers can quickly reduce the number of germs but do not eliminate all types of germs.
—*Centers for Disease Control and Prevention*

 I promote **good personal habits** with this catchy song!

(sung to the tune of "The Wheels on the Bus")

This is the way we [wash our hands],
[Wash our hands], [wash our hands].
This is the way we [wash our hands]
So that we stay healthy.

Continue with the following: *brush our teeth, cover our sneeze, wash our hair*

Rebecca Schumer, Listen and Talk, Seattle, WA

 I sing this cute song with my youngsters to remind them what to do **when they sneeze**.

(sung to the tune of "Clementine")

Get a tissue.
Get a tissue.
Get a tissue when you sneeze.
Wipe your nose and wash your hands.
Staying healthy is a breeze.

Katie Schlomer, Shepherd of the Valley Lutheran School, Westminster, CO

 I decorate each tissue box to look like a face. The nose on each box is particularly large to remind little ones to **wipe their noses** with tissues instead of sleeves!

Ruth Zabelin, Kleberg Elementary, Kingsville, TX

Problem Solved!

Your Solutions to Classroom Challenges

 I have a puppet named **Polly Polite** and a second puppet named **Bad Manners Bertha**. I share a scenario, such as "Two children want to play with the same toy." Bertha always shares a response that involves bad manners, and Polly shares a response that involves good manners. I encourage youngsters to try to explain to Bertha why Polly's option is better.

Diane Friedline, Wee Kare Early Education Center, Clinton, MA

How do you encourage *positive behavior?*

 I have each child use a **stethoscope** to listen to her heartbeat when she is calm. Whenever a youngster becomes angry, I have her listen to her heart again so she can hear that it is beating faster. Then we discuss ways she can calm her heart down. She does one of the activities until she is ready to rejoin the group.

Annie Genest, Stoneham, Quebec, Canada

 I teach children some useful **sign language** and phrases to help encourage positive behavior. One of the first signs I teach is STOP. When someone does something that a child doesn't like, he uses the sign for STOP and says, "Stop, please."

Caroline Warkentin, Lil Champions, Williams Lake, British Columbia, Canada

 To put a positive spin on behavior, I label each section of a **spinner** with a different small reward. A few times during the day, I invite a child who is demonstrating good behavior to spin the spinner.

Charla Linderer, St. Agnes Catholic Elementary, Bloomsdale, MO

 I keep a **thumbs-up** cutout near a display titled "Like or Dislike." (Many of my kids are familiar with the thumbs-up sign on Facebook!) When things are going well, I display the thumbs-up. When we are having some problems, I move the cutout so the thumb is down. Once children notice the change, they adjust their behavior.

Mary Davis, Keokuk Christian Academy, Keokuk, IA

Tattling troubles? How do you help control *tattling in your classroom?*

Your Solutions to Classroom Challenges

To keep tattling to a minimum, we begin our year with a **discussion** about what tattling is. Tattling is something done to try to get people in trouble. To assess youngsters' understanding, I give them various scenarios and students tell me whether each one is an example of tattling or not. Then I introduce the tattle bear. When a child comes to me with a tattle, I tell them to go and tell the tattle bear.

Sylvia Sonnier, Academy of the Sacred Heart, Grand Coteau, LA

I have **card props** that give my students the skills to solve their own problems instead of tattling. I put pairs of cards on separate metal rings; each ring has a bug card and a card with a magic wand (wish). When a child is doing something to upset another child and isn't causing a danger that I should know about, the upset youngster picks up a metal ring. She holds up the bug card and says, "It bugs me when you [current problem]." Then she holds up the wish card and says, "I wish you would [solution to the problem]." This method has been very effective.

Alicia Del Real, New Sullivan Elementary, Chicago, IL

I teach youngsters about **bugs** and **butterflies**. A butterfly problem is one that they can fix with their words. For example, they can say, "Please stop leaning on me" or "I don't like it when you cut in line" and the problem will "fly away" just like a butterfly. A bug problem (something dangerous) is one that stays even if words are used to try and solve it, like someone being hurt on the playground. This comparison has really helped my students grasp the concept!

Kayleigh Caldwell, Willow Creek Elementary, Nampa, ID

SCIENCE EXPLORATIONS

Science Explorations

Baked Cotton Balls

What happens when you bake cotton balls? Youngsters will be fascinated to find out with this surprising investigation!

idea contributed by Kelly Buddenhagen, Breinigsville, PA

Materials:

flour
water
plastic bowls
plastic spoons
food coloring
cotton balls
baking sheet

SETUP

Add equal parts flour and water as well as a few drops of food coloring to each bowl. Stir the mixture.

STEP 1

Gather youngsters around and show them a cotton ball. Encourage them to touch and describe the cotton ball. Then ask them what they think would happen if a cotton ball was baked in an oven. Have students share their thoughts.

STEP 2

Have each child dip cotton balls into the mixtures and then place them on a baking sheet. Bake the cotton balls for 30 to 45 minutes in a 300 degree oven. Let the cotton balls cool.

STEP 3

Encourage each youngster to explore a cotton ball, noticing that the outer texture is very hard. Then have them break open the cotton balls and investigate the soft interior texture. Finally, revisit students' predictions.

What next?

Have students use the baked cotton balls in collage projects. What a unique item to incorporate in students' arts and crafts!

Science Explorations

Will It Fit?

Youngsters need a keen sense of observation for this simple-to-prepare exploration!

idea contributed by Charlene Stull, St. Mark's Preschool
Waterford, PA

Materials:
clear plastic jar
2 trays—one labeled "Yes" and the other "No"
common items, some that fit into the jar and
    some that do not

STEP 1

Show youngsters the jar, drawing their attention to the size of the opening. Then ask them to name something that might fit through the opening and in the jar. Encourage children to share their thoughts. Then prompt students to name something that would not fit in the jar.

STEP 2

Display the items and have students identify them. Invite youngsters to handle each item, encouraging them to observe its size and shape. Ask, "Which items do you think will fit in the jar?" Have each child share her thoughts. Then ask, "Which items do you think will not fit in the jar?"

STEP 3

Set out the trays and read the labels aloud. Then ask a child to choose an item and attempt to put it in the jar. After determining whether the item will or will not fit in the jar, have her place the object on the appropriate tray. Repeat with each item.

STEP 4

Have students study the items on each tray and reflect on their predictions. Was anyone surprised to see that a certain object did fit in the jar? How about an object they thought would fit but didn't?

Try this exploration activity as a prelude to reading *The Mitten* by Jan Brett! This story is sure to spark a fun discussion about what will actually fit in a mitten.

Science Explorations

Soak It Up!

Little ones explore capillary action with some simple props!

Materials:

paper towel
copy paper
strip of lamination film
magnifying glasses
tinted water in a transparent container

watercolors
paintbrushes

STEP 1

Show youngsters the paper towel, lamination film, and copy paper. Encourage youngsters to look at the three items through a magnifying glass and discuss their similarities and differences. Ask, "What are these three things used for?" Encourage students to share their experiences with the items.

STEP 2

Next, ask, "What do you think will happen if we dip the copy paper into the water? Have students share their thoughts. Then dip the edge of the copy paper in the water and have students observe what happens, noting that the water slowly climbs up the copy paper.

STEP 3

Repeat Step 2 with the paper towel and lamination film, prompting students to notice that the water is pulled up the paper towel quickly but isn't pulled up the lamination film at all. Ask, "Do you think copy paper, lamination film, or paper towels would be better at wiping up spills? Why do you think so? Why do you think paper towels are so good at picking up water?"

STEP 4

Give each child a copy of page 129 and have her use watercolors to show what happened in the experiment.

What Next?

Get a stalk of celery with leaves and retrim the end. Then place it in a cup of tinted water. Have students observe the celery over the next few days, noting that the tinted water is pulled up into the leaves, changing their color.

Science Explorations

Marbleized Eggs

What happens when you swirl an egg in tinted water and oil? Youngsters will be fascinated with the surprising results of this investigation!

idea contributed by Marie E. Cecchini, West Dundee, IL

Materials:
food coloring
egg dipper
water in a clear
    disposable cup
2 hard-boiled eggs
vegetable oil
tablespoon
paper towel

SETUP

Mix a few drops of food coloring in the cup of water.

STEP 1

Display an egg. Ask, "What do you think will happen to this egg if we put it in the colored water?" After students share, immerse the egg. After a few moments, lift the egg and discuss the color of the shell. Then set the egg aside.

STEP 2

Pour a tablespoon of vegetable oil in the tinted water. Help students notice how the oil floats on the surface. Then stir the contents, directing youngsters' attention to the oily swirls.

STEP 3

Show the second egg. Ask, "What do you think will happen to the egg if we put it in this mixture?" After students respond, immerse the egg while swirling it and then remove it and pat it with the paper towel. Display the egg and discuss the marbleized results.

What Next?

Have students dye eggs in solid colors. Then have them marbleize the eggs with contrasting colors!

Science Explorations

Making Bubbles!

Little ones investigate which common classroom items will make bubbles!

idea contributed by Shelly Post
ECSE Helping Hands Preschool
Great Bend, KS

Materials:
large container of bubble solution
bubble wand
large blue circle cutout
classroom items

STEP 1

Show students the bubble solution and the wand. Then blow several bubbles. Ask, "Why do you think I can blow a bubble with the wand?" After they share their thoughts, prompt each student to find one item in the classroom that she thinks might allow her to blow a bubble.

STEP 2

Have each child test her item with the bubble solution. If she is able to blow a bubble, have her place the item on the blue circle. If she can't use the item to blow a bubble, have her place it aside.

STEP 3

Have youngsters look at the items on the circle. Encourage them to discuss why they believe those items can be used to blow bubbles but others can't. Can they think of other items that might be used to blow bubbles?

STEP 4

Ask students to each bring an item from home that they think can be used to blow a bubble. During center time, place a container of bubble solution at a table. Then encourage youngsters to test their items.

What Next?

Bubbles are always spherical! Give each child a copy of page 130 and have her color the bubbles that are spheres and cross out the other shapes.

What Happened?

paper

paper towel

plastic

Bubble Time!

Bubbles are spheres 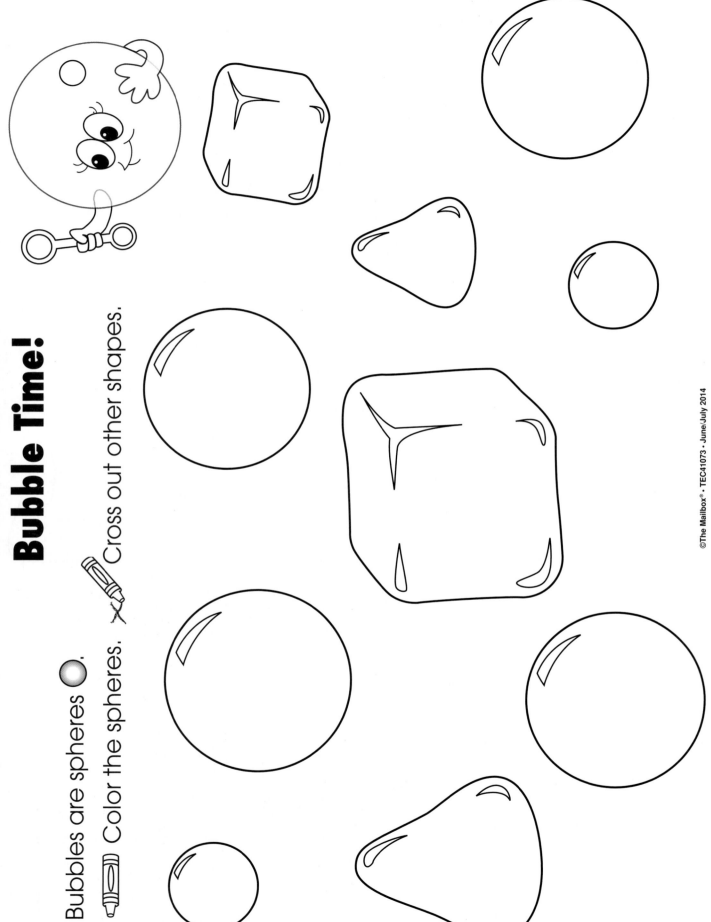.

Color the spheres.

Cross out other shapes.

Songs & Such

Songs & Such

Yum, Yum, Yum!

Spotlight sharing with this adorable apple-themed action chant! If desired, attach three felt apple cutouts to a flannelboard and remove one for each verse.

Three red apples hanging in a tree,   *Hold up three fingers.*
One fell off and landed next to me!   *Hold up one finger; then pat floor.*
I asked my friend if she wanted one.   *Pretend to hold out an apple.*
She took a bite and said, "Yum, yum, yum!"   *Pat tummy.*

Two red apples hanging in a tree,   *Hold up two fingers.*
One fell off and landed next to me.   *Hold up one finger; then pat floor.*
I asked my friend if he wanted one.   *Pretend to hold out an apple.*
He took a bite and said, "Yum, yum, yum!"   *Pat tummy.*

One red apple hanging in a tree,   *Hold up one finger.*
It fell off and landed next to me.   *Hold up one finger.*
I told my friends that I wanted one.   *Point to self.*
I took a bite and said, "Yum, yum, yum!"   *Pat tummy.*

Bonnie C. Krum
St. Matthews Early Education Center
Bowie, MD

Hello!

Here's an excellent song for greeting little ones during group time. Have youngsters stand. Then sing the song, inserting a child's name and prompting her to follow the actions. Continue with each remaining child until the entire class is seated.

(sung to the tune of "If You're Happy and You Know It")

Hello, hello, [student name]. How are you?
Hello, hello, [student name]. How are you?
Give a wiggle, wiggle, wiggle   *Wiggle hips.*
And a jiggle, jiggle, jiggle.   *Jump up and down.*
Turn around and turn around   *Turn around twice.*
And sit down.   *Sit down.*

Dee Mulranen
St. James Preschool
Aston, PA

Going on a Bus Hunt!

This twist on the traditional "Going on a Bear Hunt" chant is just perfect for the beginning of the year. Have youngsters echo each line and the actions.

Teacher: We're going on a bus hunt.	*March.*
Children: We're going on a bus hunt.	*March.*
Teacher: We're gonna find a yellow one	*Shake finger.*
Children: We're gonna find a yellow one	*Shake finger.*
Teacher: With big headlights	*Make circles with fingers.*
Children: With big headlights	*Make circles with fingers.*

Continue with the following call-and-response lines and actions:

And windshield wipers	*Swish arms back and forth.*
And big black tires.	*Point and circle arm.*
Look over there!	*Point.*
It's our bus!	*Shake finger.*
Can't go over it.	*Stand on tiptoes.*
Can't go under it.	*Crouch down.*
Can't go around it.	*Lean from side to side.*
We have to go inside it!	*Pretend to get on a bus.*

Amy Kemp, Cape Head Start, Owensville, IN

What About You?

Get to know your little ones with this chant! Recite the chant, inserting a child's name and a favorite food. Then encourage her to name her favorite food. Continue with other youngsters. If desired, substitute the favorite food with a favorite color or favorite animal.

[Child's name], [child's name],
How do you do?
I like [favorite food].
How about you?

Teresa Gleason
Village Learning Center
Somerset, KY

Songs & Such

Months of the Year

Help little ones learn the months of the year with this simple song!

(sung to the tune of "Ten Little Indians")

January, February, March, and April,
May, June, July, and August,
September, October, November, December—
These are the months of the year!

Eileen Wambach
Funshine Nursery School
Red Hook, NY

Months of the Year

January
February
March
April
May
June
July
August
September
October
November
December

Shhh!

Quiet Voices

Here's a useful little song to remind youngsters to use inside voices.

(sung to the tune of "Are You Sleeping?")

Inside voices, inside voices,
Do you hear, do you hear
Quiet, quiet voices, quiet, quiet voices?
Give a cheer, give a cheer.
Whisper: Yay!

Rita Grube
Fairlawn Preschool
Columbus, IN

Songs & Such

Fa-la-la Fall!

Spotlight fall experiences with this merry little song!

(sung to the tune of "Deck the Halls")

Rake the leaves so orange and brown.
Fa-la-la-la-la, la-la-la-fall!
Hear them make a crunching sound.
Fa-la-la-la-la, la-la-la-fall!
Pick a pumpkin; wear a sweater.
Fa-la-la, la-la-la, la-la-fall!
Birds fly south to warmer weather.
Fa-la-la-la-la, la-la-la-fall!

Jacqueline Schiff
Moline, IL

Mr. Scarecrow

What crops might Mr. Scarecrow watch over? Youngsters share their ideas with this catchy song! Have youngsters name different crops that are grown in a garden. Write down their thoughts. Then choose one of the options and lead students in singing the song, substituting the crop when indicated. Continue with different crops.

(sung to the tune of "Good Night, Ladies")

Mr. Scarecrow, Mr. Scarecrow,
Mr. Scarecrow, you guard the fields all day!
You guard [green beans], you guard [green beans],
You guard [green beans] so critters stay away!

Dawn Seigel
Evergreen Avenue School
Woodbury, NJ

P-U-M-P-K-I-N!

For extra fun, write the letters in *pumpkin* on separate pumpkin cutouts. Then attach them to a wall or board. Touch the letters when indicated as you lead youngsters in singing the song.

(sung to the tune of "Camptown Races")

P-U-M-P-K-I-N,
Pumpkin, pumpkin,
P-U-M-P-K-I-N,
Pumpkin is the word!
Pumpkins grow on vines!
Pumpkin pie is fine!
P-U-M-P-K-I-N,
Pumpkin is the word!

Susan Flener
Children's Circle—Second Presbyterian Church
Indianapolis, IN

Not So Scary!

This adorable chant is sure to be a hit with your little ones! Recite the chant. In the first blank, insert a word that rhymes with a child's name and begins with /b/. In the second blank, substitute the child's name. If desired, make a cute and cuddly sock puppet or bag puppet monster. Then use the puppet to pantomime scaring youngsters and yourself as indicated in the chant.

Bibbity Bobbity Boo—a monster scared you!
Bibbity Bobbity Bee—a monster scared me!
Bibbity Bobbity [Bessica]—a monster scared [Jessica]!

Toni Adams
Heart of Holmen Day Care
Holmen, WI

Five Little Squirrels

Here's an adorable fingerplay that's sure to be a hit with your youngsters!

Five little squirrels sat up in a tree.	*Hold up five fingers.*
This little squirrel asked, "What do you see?"	*Touch the thumb.*
This little squirrel said, "My eyes are shut!"	*Touch the index finger.*
This little squirrel said, "I'm looking for a nut!"	*Touch the middle finger.*
This little squirrel said, "One fell on my head!"	*Touch the ring finger and then clap hands.*
This little squirrel said, "Let's just go to bed."	*Touch the pinkie finger and then fold hands as if sleeping.*
Then "whoo" went the owl and rustle went the leaves,	*Flap arms and then rub hands together.*
And five little squirrels scampered down the tree!	*Wiggle fingers.*

Lori Sazinski
Bright Beginnings
Plantsville, CT

Turkey Talk

Add some action to this cute little rhyme by encouraging students to flap their arms as if they were wings whenever they hear "Gobble, gobble."

"Gobble, gobble," said the turkey.
"Gobble, gobble," said I.
"Gobble, gobble," said the turkey.
"Let's have some pie!"

"Gobble, gobble," said the turkey.
"Gobble, gobble," said you.
"Gobble, gobble," said the turkey.
"And some whipped cream too!"

Marie E. Cecchini
West Dundee, IL

Songs & Such

Perky Penguins!

This adorable fingerplay will be popular with your little ones!

Five perky penguins trek through the snow.
Two go fast, and three go slow.

Diving, sliding all day through—
That's what two fast penguins do.
Toddling, waddling every day—
That's how three slow penguins play.

Hold up hand and wave back and forth.
Hold up two fingers on one hand and
* three on the other.*
Swoop appropriate hand through the air.

Wave appropriate hand back and forth.

Betty Silkunas, Lower Gwynedd Elementary, Ambler, PA

Silent Snowflakes

Here's a chilly chant just perfect for a snowy day!

Here is a snowflake
Up in a cloud.
It doesn't shout
Or sing very loud.
In winter's cold,
Without a sound,
It softly and silently
Falls to the ground.
Fal-ling, fal-ling, on-to the ground!

Wiggle fingers high overhead.
Lower wiggling fingers slightly.
Continue lowering finger for each subsequent line.

Settle hand in lap.
Repeat descent of the snowflake with your hand.

C. Welwood, Learning Experience, Calgary, Alberta, Canada

tip To make this into a song, sing each line on a single note, beginning with a high note on the first line and getting lower with each successive line. For the final line of the song, lead students in repeating the notes sung, changing pitches for each syllable.

Santa's at the Pole!

This Christmas version of the traditional game to the song of "The Farmer in the Dell" is perfect for the season! To begin, have students stand in a circle. Then choose a child to be Santa and stand in the middle of the circle. Sing the first verse of the song, prompting students to march around the circle. Sing the second verse. Then have Santa pick a classmate to be an elf and join him in the middle of the circle. Continue in the same way with each verse. After the final verse is sung, have everyone blow a kiss to the final child chosen.

(sung to the tune of "The Farmer in the Dell")

[Santa's at the Pole. Santa's at the Pole].
Ho, ho, ho, ho, ho, ho!
[Santa's at the Pole].

Continue with the following: *Santa picks an elf, The elf picks a reindeer, The reindeer picks a sleigh, The sleigh picks a house, The house picks a chimney, The chimney picks a stocking, The stocking picks a toy, The toy picks a child, The child gets the kisses*

Faith Hann
Harmony Township School
Phillipsburg, NJ

A Holiday Tree

Reinforce color names with this catchy holiday song! Draw a simple evergreen tree on a sheet of chart paper (or on your board). Use a bingo dauber to make a red dot (light) on the tree. Have children identify the color of the light. Then lead them in singing the song shown. Continue in the same way, adding colorful lights to the tree and altering the verse each time to reflect the color name.

(sung to the tune of "Mary Wore Her Red Dress")

The pine tree has a [red] light,
A [red] light, a [red] light.
The pine tree has a [red] light
Shining bright!

Nancy Hilbert, Sonbeam Preschool, McKeesport, PA

Songs & Such

Four Little Bells

Gather four large jingle bells for this engaging winter chant! Twist a pipe cleaner (handle) into the hanger of each bell. Then give each bell to a different child and have him hold the handle. Guide students in reciting the chant, prompting each child to ring his bell after each appropriate line. Then have youngsters ring all four bells during the final two lines. Collect the bells for safekeeping.

The first bell's ring was fast.
The second bell's ring was slow.
The third bell's ring was loud.
The fourth bell's ring was low.
Then four little bells rang all together
To celebrate the winter weather!

Marie E. Cecchini
West Dundee, IL

Where Will It Land?

Give each child a snowflake die-cut for this active winter song! Then lead students in singing the song, placing the snowflake on the appropriate body part.

(sung to the tune of "London Bridge")

Little snowflake twirling round,
Twirling round, twirling round!
Little snowflake twirling round
Lands on my [head]!

Continue with the following: *knee, foot, hand, chin, leg, nose, ear, arm*

Paula Bosshart
Carpentersville, IL

Songs & Such

Old MacDonald's Pets

Spotlight pets with this snappy song! Lead students in singing the song shown and have them pretend to wiggle their tails when indicated. Continue with the other verses, having students flap their arms, run in place, pucker their lips, and pretend to dig.

(sung to the tune of "Old MacDonald Had a Farm")

Old MacDonald had a [cat]. *E-I-E-I-O!*
[And on that cat, there was a tail]. *E-I-E-I-O!*
With a [twitch, twitch] here   *Wiggle hips.*
And a [twitch, twitch] there.   *Wiggle hips.*
Here a [twitch], there a [twitch],   *Wiggle hips.*
Everywhere a [twitch, twitch].   *Wiggle hips.*
Old MacDonald had a [cat]. *E-I-E-I-O!*

Continue with the following:
*parrot; And on its sides, there were some wings; flap, flap
hamster; And in its cage, there was a wheel; run, run
fish; And on its face, there were some lips; pucker, pucker
dog; And on its legs, there were some paws; dig, dig*

Diane Simmons, Coventry, RI

Valentines for You!

To make a fun prop for this song, attach small heart cutouts to the fingers of two gloves. Then put on the gloves. Lead students in singing the song, holding up each finger when appropriate.

(sung to the tune of "Ten Little Indians")

One little, two little, three little valentines;
Four little, five little, six little valentines;
Seven little, eight little, nine little valentines;
Lots of love for you!   *Hug self and then
                                         point to a classmate.*

Jeanne-Marie Peterson, Charlottesville, VA

Cover When You Cough!

Here's a catchy song to help youngsters remember to cough or sneeze into their arms! After explaining to youngsters how to cough into their arms, lead them in singing the song. Repeat the song, replacing the word *cough* with *sneeze*.

(sung to the tune of "If You're Happy and You Know It")

Do I [cough] into the air? No, I don't!
Do I [cough] into the air? No, I don't!
All the germs go everywhere,
When I [cough] into the air.
Do I [cough] into the air? No, I don't!

Do I [cough] into my arm? Yes, I do!
Do I [cough] into my arm? Yes, I do!
When I [cough] into my arm,
All the germs can do no harm.
Do I [cough] into my arm? Yes, I do!

Nancy Howland, Little Miss Ladybug Preschool, Davenport, IA

Happy Birthday, Dr. Seuss!

Here's a fun way to kick off a Dr. Seuss birthday celebration!

(sung to the tune of "This Old Man")

Dr. Seuss,
He is fun!
He wrote books for everyone
About cats in hats
And lots of singing Whos.
Happy birthday, Dr. Seuss!

Daisy Joy, PS 290, Brooklyn, NY

Songs & Such

Lions and Lambs

Divide youngsters into two groups: lions and lambs. Then lead students in singing the song. When children hear their animal's name, prompt them to stand quickly and then sit back down. Little ones will love this active song!

(sung to the tune of "For He's a Jolly Good Fellow")

March comes in like a **lion**. March comes in like a **lion**.
March comes in like a **lion** and goes out like a **lamb**.
It goes out like a **lamb**. It goes out like a **lamb**.
March comes in like a **lion**. March comes in like a **lion**.
March comes in like a **lion** and goes out like a **lamb**!

Christine Vohs
College Church Preschool
Olathe, KS

Found a Clover

Your little ones will feel lucky indeed when they sing this fun little song! If desired, give each youngster a four-leaf clover cutout and encourage him to hold it and sway from side to side as he sings.

(sung to the tune of "Clementine")

Found a clover,
Found a clover,
Found a clover
Just for me.
It's my lucky four-leaf clover—
Found it over by the tree.

It was right there,
It was right there,
It was right there
Just for me.
With my lucky four-leaf clover,
Now I'm lucky as can be!

Cindy Hoying, Centerville, OH

Songs & Such

Five Little Kites

Program five kite cutouts for flannelboard use. Then lead students in reciting the rhyme below while you place the kites in a row on the board. Finally, give youngsters ordinal number practice by having them point to specific kites. (For example, say, "Point to the second kite.")

Five little kites went out to play.
The first kite said, "It's a windy day!"
The second kite said, "Look at me! Look at me!"
The third kite said, "Watch out for that tree!"
The fourth kite said, "Let's fly to the sun."
The fifth kite said, "What fun! What fun!"
Then whoosh went the wind, and it blew all the kites.
Then they danced in the sky and flew out of sight!

Suzanne Moore
Tucson, AZ

A Frog on a Log

Little ones will be hopping with excitement when they perform this fingerplay!

A little frog sat on a log,	*Hold up hand so it resembles a frog mouth.*
As quiet as can be.	
He didn't move. He didn't croak.	
He didn't notice me.	
By and by, a little fly	*Wiggle index finger of other hand.*
Came buzzing to and fro.	*Move finger (fly) toward the frog's mouth.*
A tongue shot out; I looked again.	*Make the frog's mouth "eat" the fly.*
Now where did that fly go?	*Hold hands behind back.*

Marie E. Cecchini
West Dundee, IL

The Thunder Song

Help youngsters feel better about thunderstorms with this soothing song!

(sung to the tune of "Twinkle, Twinkle, Little Star")

Thunder, thunder, in the sky,
Thunder never makes me cry.
Thunder's just a great big noise,
No more loud than girls and boys.
There's no need to run or hide.
You are nice and safe inside.

Tammy Tracey
Ashland Preschool Center
Cockeysville, MD

Go, Slow, Stop!

Give each child a paper plate steering wheel and lead them in singing the first verse of the song while they pretend to drive around the room. During the second verse, have them drive slowly; then have them sing the third verse while stopped.

(sung to the tune of "The Wheels on the Bus")

The [green] traffic light means [go, go, go],
[Go, go, go, go, go, go].
That is something you should know.
[Green] means [go].

Continue with the following: *yellow, slow; red, stop*

Cindy Hoying
Centerville, OH

I'm a Daffodil!

Show youngsters a flower bulb before encouraging them to perform this fun action chant!

I'm a little bulb growing in the ground.
Here are my roots going down, down, down.
Up, up, up goes my stem until—
Pop goes my bud. I'm a daffodil!

Stand still.
Slowly sink to the floor.
Raise arms up slowly.
Clap hands on "pop."

Mary Ann Craven
Fallbrook United Methodist Christian School
Fallbrook, CA

Thank You, Mom

This song is adorable when performed at a Mother's Day tea!

(sung to the tune of "Three Blind Mice")

Mother's Day,
Mother's Day,
Time to say,
Time to say
Thank you, Mom, for the things that you do.
You love me and care for me all the year through.
You are a sweet mom, and I'm thankful for you!
It's Mother's Day.

Cindy Hoying
Centerville, OH

Songs & Such

Motion in the Ocean

This adorable ocean-themed song is sure to be a favorite with your little ones!

(sung to the tune of "If You're Happy and You Know It")

There is motion in the ocean; yes, there is!
There is motion in the ocean; yes, there is!
The ocean is all brimming
Full of animals all swimming!
There is motion in the ocean; yes, there is!

Cindy Hoying, Centerville, OH

For extra fun, have each child wiggle a blue crepe paper streamer as he sings!

Five Little Trucks

Here's a truck-themed rhyme that's excellent on its own or with a transportation unit! If desired, gather five toy trucks and place them in a line. Then recite the rhyme and have a youngster make each truck "zoom away" when indicated.

Five little trucks sitting by the garage door.
One zoomed away, and then there were four.
Four little trucks as shiny as can be.
One zoomed away, and then there were three.
Three little trucks so bright and new.
One zoomed away, and then there were two.
Two little trucks parked in the sun.
One zoomed away, and then there was one.
One little truck standing all alone
Revved up its engine and headed on home.

Rosemarie Visconti
Cypress, TN

Flashing Fireflies

This quick little rhyme is a tongue twister and a study of the /f/ sound!

Five flitting fireflies
Flashing in the night.
Flicker, flicker, fireflies.
Flash your little lights!

Tricia Kylene Brown
Bowling Green, KY

tip → Transform this poem into an art project! A child mounts the poem on a sheet of black paper, presses a finger in yellow paint, and then makes five prints below the poem. Next, have her use a gold or white gel pen to make wings on each print. Finally, have her add a drop of glue to each print and then sprinkle gold glitter over the glue.

Shining Yellow Sun!

That warm, bright sunshine feels so good on a summer day! Spotlight that feeling with this song.

(sung to the tune of "Twinkle, Twinkle, Little Star")

Bright and shining yellow sun
Giving warmth to everyone.
Warming air and warming ground.
I'm so glad that you're around.
Bright and shining yellow sun
Giving warmth to everyone.

Cindy Hoying
Centerville, OH

STORYTIME

Storytime

Literacy Ideas for Teachers®

Shapes, Shapes, Shapes

By Tana Hoban

Shapes are everywhere! This wordless book full of vivid photographs shows a variety of shapes in everyday items and structures.

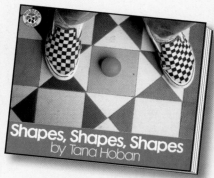

● ● ● **Before You Read** ● ● ●

Make a few brightly colored shape cutouts. Then attach them in your room near items that are the same shape. For example, attach a circle next to a round clock and a rectangle on your door. Make sure the shapes are visible from your group-time area. To begin, have children scan the room for shape cutouts. When a child notices one, prompt him to identify it. Then say, "Oh my goodness! This [circle] is right next to the [clock], and the [clock] is also a [circle]!" Continue with the other shapes. Then say, "The book we're going to look at has a lot of different shapes in places you wouldn't think to look for them!" ***Shapes in the environment***

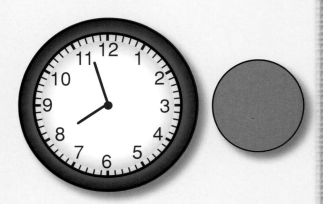

● ● ● **After You Read** ● ● ●

Provide a variety of traceable items in different shapes, such as a tissue box, a wooden block, a pan lid, and a plastic container. Encourage youngsters to notice that the items are different shapes. Prompt them to identify the shapes. Then encourage them to trace the items on a sheet of paper and color or paint the tracings as desired. ***Identifying shapes***

Duck & Goose

By Tad Hills

Duck and Goose find what they believe to be an egg. They squabble over which one of them will sit on it, which one of them will teach the baby inside to swim, and whether the baby will quack or honk. Soon Duck and Goose realize that this egg really isn't an egg at all. It's a ball!

ideas contributed by Ada Goren
Winston-Salem, NC

Duck	Goose	Other
X	X	X
X	X	X
X		
X		

● ● ● ● **Before You Read** ● ● ● ●

Show students the book cover and explain that Duck and Goose believe that they are sitting on an egg. Ask youngsters what they predict will hatch from the egg. Will it be a duck, a goose, or something else? If desired, record youngsters' predictions on a chart as shown. Then read the story aloud. ***Predicting, graphing***

● ● ● ● **After You Read** ● ● ● ●

Now Duck and Goose have to share the ball! Show youngsters a playground ball. Then call on a child and ask her how the two of you could share the ball, such as by rolling it back and forth, playing catch with it, or taking turns bouncing it. Have students demonstrate each example. Then ask, "Do you think Duck and Goose will do a good job sharing the ball?" Prompt youngsters to explain their thinking. ***Speaking***

Leonardo the Terrible Monster

By Mo Willems

Leonardo is a monster—just not a very good one. No matter what he does, he just can't seem to frighten anyone. Then along comes Sam. Leonardo is convinced he can scare the tuna salad out of Sam, but he ends up befriending him instead!

ideas contributed by Tricia Kylene Brown, Bowling Green, KY

● ● ● Before You Read ● ● ●

Two! You're not very scary!

To prepare youngsters for this not-so-scary story, ask, "Do you think monsters are real or make-believe?" After students share their thoughts, reassure them that monsters are make-believe; then turn down the lights for some monster-style fun! With children facing away from you, quietly sneak up behind the group and do your scariest monster impression. Then ask children to rate how scary you are—one for scary and two for not-so-scary—to see if you would make a good monster or a terrible monster. Then have little ones settle in for this comical read-aloud with a delightful ending!
Differentiating between real and make-believe

● ● ● After You Read ● ● ●

Have each student make her own scary or not-so-scary monster with this activity. Set out colorful construction paper shapes, assorted craft materials, markers, and glue. Encourage each youngster to use desired shapes to create a monster head and body. Then have her use the remaining materials to add monster-like details. When the projects are finished, invite little ones to help their monsters try to scare the tuna salad out of you! **Responding to a story through art**

Thanks for Thanksgiving

Written by Julie Markes
Illustrated by Doris Barrette

The rhythmic text and captivating illustrations throughout the pages of this book are thoughtful reminders of simple, everyday things for which to be truly thankful.

I am thankful for my new puppy!

● ● ● Before You Read ● ● ●

Have students sit in a circle. Briefly discuss what it means to be thankful; then have youngsters pass a beanbag (turkey) around the circle as you lead them in chanting, "Family, homes, or friends galore—tell us what you're thankful for!" At the end of the chant, have the child holding the turkey tell something she's thankful for. Continue until each child has had a turn to speak; then read the story aloud to see if the things youngsters are thankful for are mentioned in the book. ***Speaking to share information***

● ● ● After You Read ● ● ●

Review the covers and pages of the book, encouraging youngsters to notice picture details that are reminiscent of things in their lives. Next, give each child a copy of page 162 and invite him to draw something in the oval for which he is thankful. Have him dictate words for you to write below the oval; then invite him to add holiday-related stickers to the page. If desired, mount the page on fall-colored paper and then send it home as a Thanksgiving Day memento! ***Dictating information***

A Peek at What I'm Thankful For!

I am thankful for my nana's chocolate chip cookies!

by **Ian**

Storytime

Literacy Ideas for Teachers®

Too Many Toys

By David Shannon

Spencer's humongous toy collection becomes such an annoying and dangerous nuisance that his mother decides some toys just have to go. This decision leads to a frenzy of negotiating about downsizing the inventory because, according to Spencer, every toy is his favorite.

ideas contributed by Tricia Kylene Brown, Bowling Green, KY

● ● ● Before You Read ● ● ●

Spill a sack of classroom toys onto the floor and ask, "If we had toys sprawled out all over the classroom floor like this, would it be safe?" Encourage each child to share her thoughts; then elicit students' help in cleaning up the toys. Next, ask, "Do you know anyone who has toys all over his or her floor?" After a brief discussion, tell youngsters that today's story is about a boy who has so many toys they mess up the whole house. Then read this eye-opening tale aloud. **Building prior knowledge**

It would hurt to step on those toys!

● ● ● After You Read ● ● ●

Ask youngsters what they think about Spencer's mother's decision to get rid of some of his toys. Was it a fair decision? Why? After a brief discussion, set out the toys from "Before You Read" along with two containers: one labeled "stays" and the other "goes." Invite youngsters to pretend they have to decide which toys to keep and which ones must go. Then prompt them to make decisions about each toy. Encourage students to talk through the decision-making process and tell how they might feel if they actually had to get rid of the toys. Finally, ask, "What are some things we could do with the toys that we decided not to keep?" **Speaking**

Snow

Written by Cynthia Rylant
Illustrated by Lauren Stringer

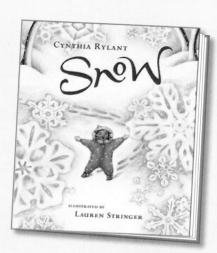

The lyrical text and captivating illustrations throughout this book joyfully celebrate the wonders of snow—from light snow to heavy snow to the quiet snow that falls in the night.

● ● ● Before You Read ● ● ●

Show youngsters the cover of the book and explain that the book talks about different kinds of snow. Say, "Some snowflakes are very large and heavy." Then encourage students to stand and move like heavy snowflakes. Next, say, "Some snowflakes are very light." Then prompt students to move like light snowflakes. Finally, say, "Some snowflakes blow around and around before settling down." Then have youngsters move this way and that as they pretend to be blowing snowflakes. Encourage your little snowflakes to settle in for a reading of this whimsical and nostalgic book. ***Gross-motor skills***

After You Read ● ● ●

Review pages of the book that personify the snow with characteristics like "shy friend" and "cheerful" flakes. Then invite each child to create a snowflake with a personality of its own! Set out construction paper copies of page 163 and craft materials, like wiggle eyes, cotton batting, yarn, paper scraps, markers, and glue. Encourage each child to decorate a snowflake to show some personality; then have her dictate something about the snowflake. If desired, display the projects along with the title "Snowflakes With Personality!" ***Writing, extending a story***

Snowflakes With Personality!

My snowflake is very happy. It blows around and around really fast, and then it sits on my house.

Literacy Ideas for Teachers®

The Magic Hat

Written by Mem Fox
Illustrated by Tricia Tusa

One fine day, a magic hat appears in the sky. It tumbles and bounces through the air and makes magic wherever it lands. Everyone is delighted as, one by one, the townspeople are transformed into giant playful animals. And then a wizard arrives…

ideas contributed by Ada Goren
Lewisville, NC

● ● ● Before You Read ● ● ●

Show students the book cover and read the title aloud. Pass a hat to a youngster and invite him to share what he thinks the magic hat in the story will be able to do. Continue in this manner until each child has made a prediction. Then read the story aloud to find out if any of the predictions are correct! **Predicting**

If the magic hat landed on [Charlie]'s head, he would be…

If the magic hat landed on [Charlie]'s head, he would be…

an elephant!

● ● ● After You Read ● ● ●

Which animals would youngsters become if the magic hat landed on their heads? Program a sheet of paper with the prompt shown and make a copy for each child. Have him attach a large index card to a sheet of programmed paper to make a flap. Have each child cut an animal picture from a nature magazine (or draw a picture of an animal) and glue it beneath the flap. Write the name of the animal on the page. Then, on the flap, have him glue a full-length photo of himself wearing a hat. Bind the pages between two covers and then read the class book aloud. **Making a class book**

The Napping House

Written by Audrey Wood
Illustrated by Don Wood

As rain falls, a granny is snoring on her cozy bed while a child and animals doze nearby. One by one, the nappers make their way to the granny's bed, and each finds a comfortable spot in which to sleep. Then a tiny flea joins the pile of snoozing pals and sets off a wild, wide-awake chain of events.

ideas contributed by Ada Goren
Lewisville, NC

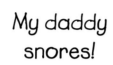

My daddy snores!

● ● ● Before You Read ● ● ●

Gather students and tell them that the book you are going to read is about a houseful of people and animals that are taking a nap on a rainy day. Explain that one of the characters in the story snores. Invite each child, in turn, to make a loud snore and then share what she knows about snoring. After everyone has shared, read the story aloud. **Oral language**

● ● ● After You Read ● ● ●

To prepare, make a flea wand like the one shown. Revisit the pages of the story where the flea's actions cause the napping animals and people to wake up. Discuss how the characters might have felt when they were awakened. Have youngsters pretend to sleep as you lead them in saying the rhyme shown. At the end of the rhyme, tap a child on the shoulder with the flea wand. Have her "wake up" with great dramatic flair. Continue until everyone has had a turn. **Making connections**

Look out for that little flea!
I wonder if he'll come wake me?

Storytime

Literacy Ideas for Teachers®

How to Catch a Star
By Oliver Jeffers

The boy in this story loves stars too much to simply gaze at them—he wants to catch one of his own! After several valiant yet failed attempts, he unexpectedly catches a beautiful star as he walks home along the beach.

ideas contributed by Janet Boyce, Cokato, MN

● ● ● **Before You Read** ● ● ●

To prepare, suspend a die-cut star from the ceiling or post it on a wall. Also get a working flashlight. Display the cover of the book and read its title aloud. Tell youngsters that today's story is about a little boy who desperately wants to catch a star. Then dim the lights and shine the flashlight on the die-cut. Ask, "What would you do to try and catch a star?" After little ones share their thoughts, read the story aloud so students can see if the things they would try are mentioned in the book. ***Speaking to share information***

I would fly on a rocket to catch a star!

● ● ● **After You Read** ● ● ●

Hide a class supply of die-cut stars in your sand table. Also place squeeze bottles of glue and a container of sand at a table. (If desired, make colorful sand by mixing it with powdered tempera paint.) Invite each child to find a star in the sand just like the little boy in the story did. Encourage the child to squeeze glue onto the star and then sprinkle sand on the glue. When the glue is dry, mount the stars on a beach-themed display with the title "I Can Catch a Star!" ***Fine-motor skills***

Minerva Louise and the Colorful Eggs

By Janet Morgan Stoeke

Perched on a fence, Minerva Louise basks in the splendor of springtime. Then she discovers a blue egg and sets off to find its mother, which leads her to an array of other colorful eggs. Baffled by what she sees, she elicits the help of other curious hens to solve this colorful mystery!

One egg is an Easter egg!

● ● ● **Before You Read** ● ● ●

Display a basket containing a white egg and a colorfully decorated egg. Invite youngsters to tell how the eggs are different and ways they might be used. Then show the cover of the book and encourage students to describe the scene. Draw youngsters' attention to the egg and invite each child to predict what happens in the story. Then have little ones settle in for a read-aloud of this comical mystery! *Visual discrimination, speaking to share information, predicting*

Sam finds a colorful egg!

● ● ● **After You Read** ● ● ●

Hide a class supply of egg cutouts around the classroom. Direct each child to find one egg and then have him decorate it using markers and stickers. When he's finished, have him glue the egg to a sheet of construction paper programmed as shown. Next, print a photo of each child sitting and then cut out the photos. Have each child glue his photo to his egg as if he is sitting on it! Bind the pages together and title the book "[Teacher name]'s Class and the Colorful Eggs!" *Responding to a story through art, creating a class book*

 See page 164 for a **reproducible** that helps youngsters recall story details!

Storytime

Literacy Ideas for Teachers®

Wet Dog!
Written by Elise Broach
Illustrated by David Catrow

A lovable, good old dog is looking for relief on a very hot day. But every time this shaggy pooch finds a way to cool off, he gets shooed away! A baby helps people realize that this old dog has the right idea.

ideas contributed by Janet Boyce, Cokato, MN

● ● ● Before You Read ● ● ●

Display the cover of the book and read its title aloud. Ask, "Does anyone know how a wet dog dries itself?" After youngsters respond, have them pretend to be puppies. "Spray" the puppies with a hose and then prompt them to shake off the water. When the puppies are dry, have them settle in for this tail-wagging read-aloud. Be sure to encourage each pup to "pat-a-pat" his legs and "shaky-shake" his body at the appropriate times during the story! ***Activating prior knowledge, gross-motor skills***

● ● ● After You Read ● ● ●

Invite each child to make her own wet dog! Encourage her to draw a dog on a sheet of paper. When she's finished, have her dip a small paintbrush in blue-tinted water and then shake it over the picture. Have her repeat the process several times so it looks like the dog is shaking itself dry! ***Responding to a story through art***

Jamberry
By Bruce Degen

Follow a lovable bear and his boy companion through their adventures in an imaginary berry-filled land. Captivating rhymes and detailed illustrations are sure to leave youngsters hungry for repeated readings of this story!

ideas by Janet Boyce, Cokato, MN

> I went strawberry picking with my grandpa!

● ● ● **Before You Read** ● ● ●

To prepare, fill each of several bowls with a different color of pom-poms (berries). To begin, ask, "Has anyone ever gone berry picking? If so, what kind of berries did you pick?" After little ones share, display a bowl of berries. Have students identify the color and then give the berries a name. Repeat with the other bowls of berries and then read aloud this jam-packed, berry-picking adventure!
Speaking to share information

After You Read ● ● ●

Help youngsters make a no-cook strawberry jam using the recipe shown. Then provide crackers, paper plates, and plastic knives and invite little ones to enjoy a delicious jam and cracker snack! ***Following directions***

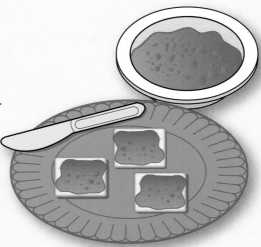

Ingredients
1.59 oz. package instant fruit pectin
1½ c. sugar
4 c. mashed frozen strawberries

Directions
Mix the pectin and sugar in a large bowl. Add the strawberries and stir for three minutes. Allow the jam to stand for 30 minutes before serving. Cover and refrigerate any leftover jam.

A Peek at What I'm Thankful For!

by _____

Note to the teacher: Use with "After You Read" on page 153.

Snowflakes With Personality!

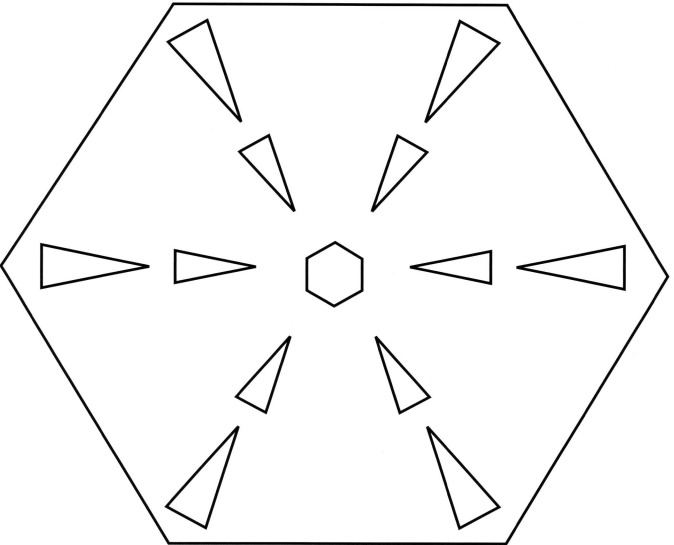

Note to the teacher: Use with "After You Read" on page 155.

THE MAILBOX **163**

Minerva Louise and the Colorful Eggs

by Janet Morgan Stoeke

What did you see in the story?

Note to the teacher: Use with "*Minerva Louise and the Colorful Eggs*" on page 159. Give each child a copy of the page. Then have her identify the pictures and point to or color the ones that were in the story.

BOOK UNITS

I Like Myself!

Written by Karen Beaumont
Illustrated by David Catrow

The youngster in this story likes herself from her nose down to her toes. Even if she had fleas or warts or a "silly snout that snorts," she would still be herself. And that's who she wants to be!

ideas created by Roxanne LaBell Dearman
NC Early Intervention Program for Children Who Are Deaf or Hard of Hearing
Charlotte, NC

A "Me" Booklet!
Print awareness

The little girl in the book likes all her parts, from her nose to her toes. Youngsters celebrate their parts with a booklet that incorporates printmaking! Make a copy of the booklet pages on pages 167 and 168 for each child. Then, on booklet pages 1–3, help each youngster use paint to make a print of the body part mentioned. Have him draw a picture of himself on the final page. When the paint is dry, help him cut out his pages and staple them behind a cover titled "I Like Me!"

Let's Discuss

Engage little ones in brief conversations about the ideas presented in the book!

- Show youngsters the page that shows the little boy making fun of the girl. Read the text on the page. Ask, "Has anyone ever said something that hurt your feelings?" Encourage youngsters to share their experiences.
- Show students the page that shows the little girl looking messy in the morning. Say, "Tell me about a time when you were a mess. What were you doing?"
- Ask, "What do you like about yourself?"

A Song About Me!

Give each child an *M* card and an *E* card. Have each student place the cards on the floor in front of her. Then lead youngsters in singing the song, pointing to the letters when indicated and then pointing to themselves when they say "me."

(sung to the tune of "Bingo")

I like my nose; I like my toes.
I really like to be me.
M, E—I like me!
M, E—I like me!
M, E—I like me!
That's who I want to be!
Shout: Me!

2

I like my knee.

1

I like my hand.

4

I like me!

3

I like my toes.

The Little Yellow Leaf

Written and illustrated by Carin Berger

As the other leaves float past Little Yellow Leaf, he thinks, "I'm not ready yet." The seasons change all around, but Little Yellow Leaf still hangs on. When the snow starts to fall, he notices a little red leaf hanging on above him. Perhaps they can let go together.

ideas contributed by Elizabeth Cook
Glendale Lutheran Early Learning Center, Glendale, MO

A Leafy Performance
Participating in a reenactment

This simple story is perfect for a dramatic retelling! Prepare a few brown leaf cutouts, one yellow leaf cutout, and one red leaf cutout. After reading the story, invite a child to be the tree. Then distribute the leaves and direct the youngsters with leaves to take their places near the tree. As you do a simple retelling of the story, have little ones act out their assigned parts. Repeat the activity until each child has had a turn to play a part.

Plenty of Paper
Creating a collage

In advance, gather a large supply of paper scraps. (Consider gathering a variety of types, such as scrapbook paper, newspaper, magazine pages, receipts, and lined paper.) Revisit the illustrations, guiding students to notice the different types of paper used. Set out all the paper scraps and invite youngsters to help you sort them. Then place the paper scraps, scissors, and glue near a table with a length of bulletin board paper. Invite small groups of youngsters to join you at the table and cut or tear paper scraps and glue them to the bulletin board paper to create a scene or a freestyle collage. After each child has added to the artwork, display it.

tip → Do your youngsters have parents that do scrapbooking as a hobby? Scrapbookers **always** have oodles of paper scraps. Ask them to donate their scraps for this artwork.

A View From Above
Exploring point of view

This delightful book uses aerial views of trees and fields in some of its illustrations. Encourage youngsters to look at objects from different angles with this matching game. Choose several objects and then take two photos—one straight on and one from above—of each object. Enlarge and print the photos. Then scatter the aerial view photos on the floor and keep the straight-on photos nearby. Give a child a straight-on photo. Then encourage him to identify the item and find its matching bird's-eye view. Continue until all the photos are matched.

Seasonal Changes
Using text and illustrations to support answers

Prior to a second reading of the story, explain to little ones that even though the author does not say that the seasons are changing, we can tell from the text and illustrations that they are. Give each child a leaf die-cut. As you reread the story, invite each child to raise her leaf when she hears or sees something that tells her the seasons are changing. Ask her to share her reasoning.

Little Yellow Questions
Answering questions about a story

Cut out a yellow copy of the leaf patterns on page 171. Have youngsters sit in a circle. Then toss the yellow leaves in the middle of the circle as if they have fallen from a tree. Have a child pick up a leaf. Then read aloud the question and encourage the child to answer it. Continue with each remaining leaf.

Do you like fall? Why or why not?

Do you like the story? Why or why not?

Is it okay to not be ready to do something?

Let's pretend the red leaf isn't there. What do you think will happen?

Name something you aren't ready to do. Why aren't you ready?

Why do you think Little Yellow Leaf isn't ready?

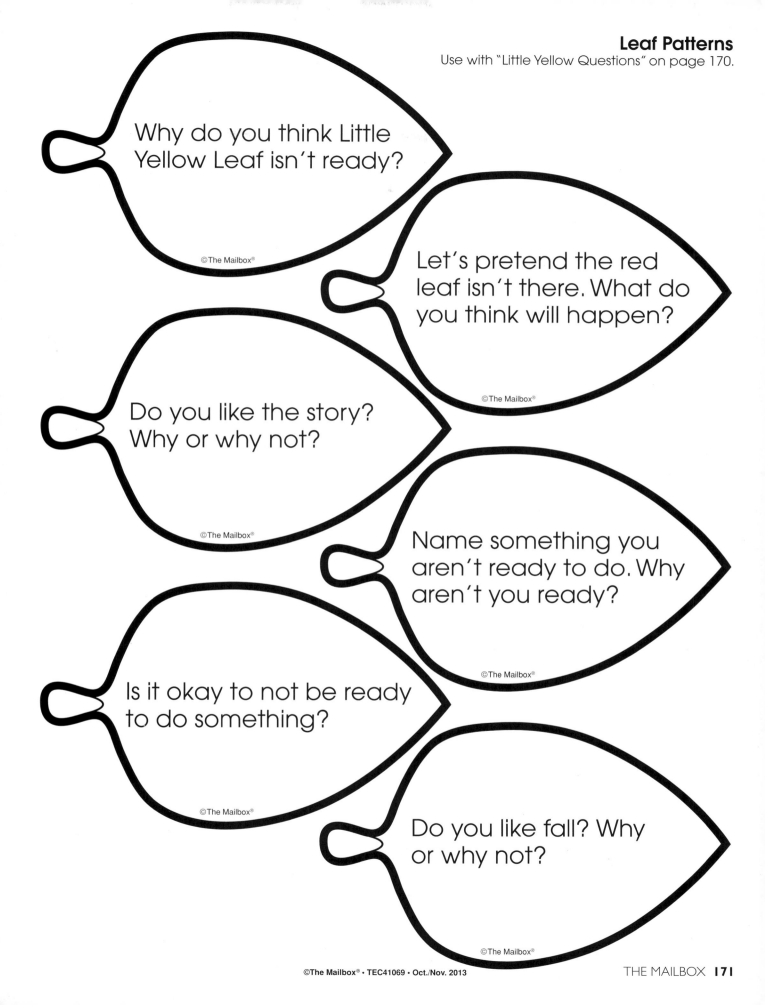

Why do you think Little Yellow Leaf isn't ready?

©The Mailbox®

Let's pretend the red leaf isn't there. What do you think will happen?

©The Mailbox®

Do you like the story? Why or why not?

©The Mailbox®

Name something you aren't ready to do. Why aren't you ready?

©The Mailbox®

Is it okay to not be ready to do something?

©The Mailbox®

Do you like fall? Why or why not?

©The Mailbox®

Unusual Chefs!

A rooster, an iguana, wild boars, and tiny construction workers!
The characters in these books are not your normal kitchen crew!

ideas contributed by Roxanne LaBell Dearman
NC Intervention for the Deaf and Hard of Hearing, Charlotte, NC

Cook-a-doodle-doo!

Written by Janet Stevens and Susan Stevens Crummel
Illustrated by Janet Stevens

Rooster and his animal assistants are going to bake his great-grandmother's strawberry shortcake recipe. But Pig wants to taste everything, and Iguana doesn't know the difference between a stick of butter and a stick from a tree. In the end, they pull together and make a lovely shortcake!

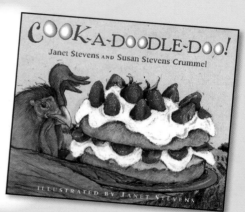

Silly Chefs!
Manipulating phonemes, rhyming

Cut out pictures of foods from a store circular and place them near a bowl. Then review the silly things the chefs in the book do, such as dig up a flower to add to the recipe instead of using flour! Next, tell youngsters that you will be a silly chef. Say, for example, "Silly Chef says to put a bapple in the bowl." After the giggles die down, have a child find a picture with a name that rhymes with *bapple* (apple) and place it in the bowl. Continue with other silly rhymes!

Build a Shortcake!
Patterning

Youngsters can make a shortcake just as they do in the story! Cut yellow or light-brown craft foam into circles to make the shortcake layers. Also, cut same-size quilt batting circles (cream) and gather red pom-poms (berries). Revisit the page that shows how the characters layer the cake. Then have a child place a shortcake layer on the floor. Ask, "What comes next?" After a child has placed a layer of cream, encourage another student to sprinkle a layer of berries. Continue guiding them to build a tall shortcake continuing the pattern.

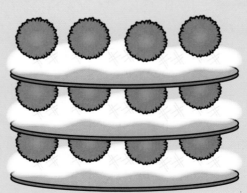

For extra fun! Place the shortcake props in a center with the book, mixing bowls, mixing spoons, circular baking pans, and measuring cups and spoons. Encourage youngsters to revisit the story and make a shortcake with the props!

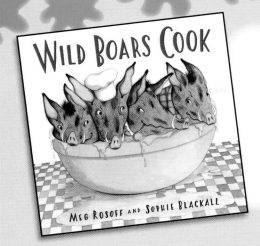

Wild Boars Cook

Written by Meg Rosoff
Illustrated by Sophie Blackall

What do wild boars put in a massive pudding? Butter, chocolates, bananas, and squid—to name just a few ingredients! And they eat the pudding until nothing is left. But the wild boars are still hungry!

Goris, Toris, and Loris?
Rhyming, creating a story innovation

The wild boars' names are Boris, Morris, Horace, and Doris. What if the wild boars had cousins coming to visit and their names rhymed as well? Have a youngster suggest a rhyming name for a wild boar cousin. Write the name on your board and say, "[Name] came to visit, and he was hungry. He saw the massive pudding and said..." Then prompt students to recite the rhyme shown. Repeat the process for a variety of different rhyming names. Then conclude the activity by saying, "And so they all ate the massive pudding!"

Crunch, crunch, crunch!
Munch, munch, munch!
Yum, yum, yum!
I want some!

May I have a banana, please?

Please and Thank You
Character education: using polite words

Do the wild boars have polite table manners? They certainly don't! But your little ones can demonstrate the correct way to behave! Put down a paper plate. Place play food in the middle of the circle. Then ask, "How would the wild boars act during dinner?" Prompt students to make dramatic munching and crunching noises. Then ask, "How would polite preschoolers act during dinner?" Give the plate to a child and encourage him to ask, "May I have a [food name], please?" Put the named food on his plate and prompt him to say, "Thank you." Continue for several rounds.

What's in the Cookie?
Responding to a story through art

Doris has her eyes on a cookie recipe for the next foodie creation. What will the boars put in the recipe? Give each child a wild boar–size cookie cutout. Have her think about what the boars would put in the cookie and then paint it as desired. Prompt the child to name the ingredients in the cookie. Write her thoughts on slips of paper and attach them to the wet paint. What fun!

stinky socks
blueberries
fish
pepperoni

 Develop story recall skills with the reproducible on page 175!

Who Made This Cake?

Written by Chihiro Nakagawa
Illustrated by Junji Koyose

When a woman orders a birthday cake for her son, a miniature construction crew with tiny bulldozers and cranes makes the cake, bakes it, and decorates it!

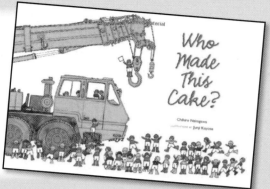

What Does It Do?
Building vocabulary, speaking

In advance, gather eggbeaters, a butter knife (for spreading frosting), a potholder, and a measuring cup with a spout for pouring. Show the pages from the book that depict the construction crew completing the tasks that would normally require these tools. Discuss what the little people are doing in the pictures. Then have students find the corresponding tools. Next, have a child choose one of the items and discuss a time he has seen someone use it. Have him put the item back. Continue in the same way with other youngsters.

Driving Decorations
Responding to a story through art

Youngsters can use construction vehicles to decorate a cake with this process art! Cut paper to fit into a 9" x 13" cake pan and provide small toy construction vehicles and shallow pans of paint. Place a piece of paper in the pan and lightly tape it in place. A child dips a construction vehicle into the paint and then rolls it onto the paper. He continues with other vehicles and colors of paint.

Build a Cake
Retelling the story

Get your sand table ready for a retelling of the story! Place small construction vehicles in your sand table along with round cake pans, candles, small "Happy Birthday" signs, strawberries cut from red craft foam, bowls, and plastic eggs. Little ones visit the center and use the items to retell the story and make a sand cake!

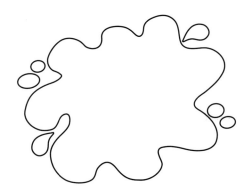

Wild Boars Cook

Written by Meg Rosoff
Illustrated by Sophie Blackall

What do the boars put in the pudding?

©The Mailbox® • TEC41070 • Dec./Jan. 2013–14

Note to the teacher: Use with "*Wild Boars Cook*" on page 173. Give a student a copy of the page and have him color the appropriate pictures.

The Gruffalo

Written by Julia Donaldson
Illustrated by Axel Scheffler

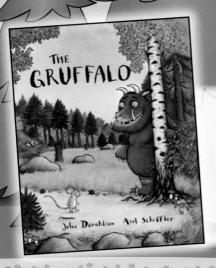

When Mouse encounters a hungry fox, he pretends he is waiting for a Gruffalo, a scary creature entirely of Mouse's imagination who loves to eat roasted fox! The fox hides, and so Mouse repeats the story to each hungry critter he meets in the woods. But what is quick-thinking Mouse to do when he actually meets a Gruffalo?

Some Scary Parts!
Organizing data

Terrible tusks, orange eyes, and a poisonous wart! Which is the scariest feature of the Gruffalo? Your youngsters will be eager to share their opinions. Make supersize tusk, orange eye, and green wart cutouts. Then attach them to a wall. Open up the book to a large picture of the Gruffalo. Have students study the picture and determine what the scariest feature is: the tusks, the eyes, or the wart. Have each child write his name (or initials) on a sticky note and attach it to the appropriate feature. Then help students count and compare the results. That's one scary critter!

Ada Goren, Lewisville, NC

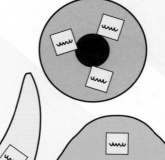
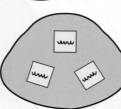

My Very Own Gruffalo
Developing fine-motor skills

When youngsters cut out features for their own Gruffalo puppet, the unique results will be adorable! To make a puppet, make a tongue cutout from black construction paper and attach it to a paper lunch bag beneath the flap. Then attach white square cutouts (teeth) on either side of the tongue. Attach two white rectangular cutouts (tusks) on top of the flap. Between the tusks, glue a brown nose cutout. Then add ear, eye, and horn cutouts as shown. Draw a green wart on the nose. Then flip the bag over and draw purple spikes on its back. So cute!

Ada Goren

Super Sound Effects!

Participating in an interactive read-aloud

Gather a set of instruments, such as a few tambourines, and give each one to a different child. Reread the story encouraging youngsters to play their tambourines dramatically every time you say the word *gruffalo*. This active read-aloud is a fun way to emphasize a unique main character!

A New Name

Phonological awareness: rhyming

Have students repeat the rhyming couplet shown. Tell them that the author wrote the words so that *know* and *gruffalo* would rhyme. Say, "Let's see if we can change the words a little and still make them rhyme." Then repeat the first line of the couplet, replacing the underlined phrase with one of the suggestions given. Continue with the second line, encouraging little ones to help you alter the word *gruffalo* to make it rhyme. You're sure to hear some giggles! Continue with each suggestion.

Silly old Fox! [Doesn't he know?]
There's no such thing as a [gruffalo]!

Suggestions:
Didn't he guess? gruffaless
Hasn't he heard? gruffalerd
He isn't smart; gruffalart
Isn't he funny? gruffalunny
He hasn't a clue; gruffaloo
He's not too bright; gruffalight

Mixed-Media Fun!

Expressing oneself through art, exploring art mediums

The illustrations in the story were created with pencils, ink, watercolors, colored pencils, and crayons. Gather the different mediums. (For the ink, consider using fine-tip permanent markers.) To begin, invite a small group to paint a sheet of paper with watercolors. Then, when the paint is dry, challenge youngsters to add to the artwork using all the remaining mediums. When they are finished, ask them which medium they enjoyed the most and which they enjoyed the least. If desired, graph the results!

 See page 178 for **story question cards!**

Question Cards

Cut out a copy of the cards and put them in a container. Have youngsters pass the container around the circle as they chant, "Gruffalo, gruffalo, there are things we want to know!" Have a child take a card. Read the question and then help the child answer it. Continue with the remaining cards.

What was the first animal the mouse met? The second? The third?

TEC41071

Why did the mouse tell the animals he was waiting for a gruffalo?

TEC41071

Were the animals really afraid of the mouse? What were they afraid of?

TEC41071

Why did the gruffalo run away from the mouse?

TEC41071

What was your favorite part of the story?

TEC41071

Where did this story take place?

TEC41071

"Moo-ving" Storytime Selections

You're sure to hear lots of giggles with these cow-themed read-alouds!

*ideas contributed by Roxanne LaBell Dearman
NC Intervention for the Deaf and Hard of Hearing
Charlotte, NC*

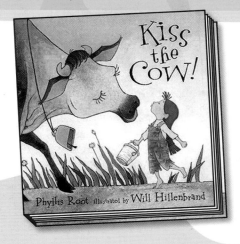

 ## Kiss the Cow!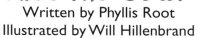
Written by Phyllis Root
Illustrated by Will Hillenbrand

Mama May has many children, and she depends on her cow, Luella, for milk. Each day, Mama says the magic words, collects the milk, and then gives Luella a kiss on the nose. Annalisa, Mama's most curious child, just has to try milking Luella herself. She remembers to say the magic words but refuses to kiss the cow. Now Luella won't give any milk until she gets her kiss!

Would You?
Graphing, sharing an opinion
Would your little ones kiss a cow like Annalisa did? You'll find out with this activity! Make a two-column graph similar to the one shown. Then give each child a cow card (see page 182). Ask each youngster to think about whether he would be willing to kiss a cow. Then have him put his card in the appropriate location on the graph. Finally, have students discuss the results of the graph.

Cow Craft
Following directions, recalling story events
These simple cow crafts are adorable! To make one, get a lip-shaped rubber stamp or cut a simple lip shape from a sponge. Paint the bottom of a paper plate light brown (or, for a quicker project, leave the plate white). Attach two white horn cutouts and two black ear cutouts to the plate. Then attach a pink oval. Use a black marker to draw a mouth, nostrils, and eyes. Next, press the stamp on a red ink pad and then press it onto the cow's nose. If desired, glue a copy of the appropriate card on page 183 to the back of the craft.

Click, Clack, Moo: Cows That Type
Written by Doreen Cronin
Illustrated by Betsy Lewin

When the cows discover an old typewriter in the barn, they type a note to Farmer Brown demanding electric blankets. After all, the barn is quite cold. When Farmer Brown refuses, they refuse to give milk. Then the hens get involved and refuse to give eggs! What's a farmer to do?

Click Clack Sounds
Creating a story innovation

Familiarize little ones with a typewriter with this before-reading activity! In advance, search "typewriter sounds" on YouTube and choose one of the many options. Also get a picture of a typewriter (or a real typewriter). Show the picture to youngsters. Ask, "Does anyone know what this is?" After several youngsters share their thoughts, explain that a typewriter is a machine that people used before computers became popular. A typewriter uses ink to make letters on paper. Further explain that a typewriter makes loud clacking noises when you use it to type. Play the YouTube video, prompting students to notice how the typewriter makes a noise that sounds like "click, clack, click, clack." Then have little ones settle in for this entertaining story!

Click, Clack, Oink!
Participating in a song, investigating animal sounds

What would it sound like if other animals started typing? After a read-aloud of the story, have youngsters sing the first verse of the song below. Next, focus students' attention on the title of the book. Say, "What if this story was about pigs? What would the title be?" Lead students to conclude that the title would be *Click, Clack, Oink*. Have little ones sing the second verse of the song. Continue with the other animals suggested.

(sung to the tune of "Mary Had a Little Lamb")

[Cows] are typing:
Click, clack, [moo],
Click, clack, [moo],
Click, clack, [moo].
[Cows] are typing:
Click, clack, [moo],
Clickety clack, [moo, moo]!

Continue with the following: *pigs, oink; ducks, quack; geese, honk; sheep, baa*

Cows Can't Fly
Written and Illustrated by David Milgrim

A little boy draws cows flying through the air and, soon after, real cows begin to soar around the town. If the townspeople would only look up instead of down, they would see a fantastic sight!

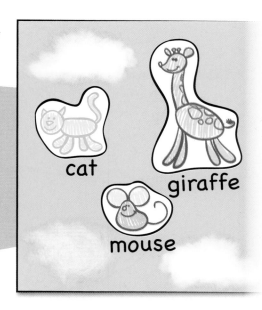

cat

giraffe

mouse

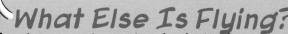

What Else Is Flying?
Creating a story innovation, developing fine-motor skills
This sky mural is truly unique! After a read-aloud of the story, have youngsters glue cotton batting (clouds) to a length of blue bulletin board paper. When the glue is dry, attach the paper to a wall. Encourage students to think of other animals that normally don't fly. Then prompt them to draw and cut out desired animals and glue them to the paper. Label each child's drawing.

Moo For True!
Distinguishing fantasy from reality
For this whole-group activity, say one of the statements below. If the sentence is a true statement about cows, have youngsters say, "Moo—that's true!" If the statement is false, have little ones pretend to fly, just like the cows in the story! Continue with each remaining statement.

Suggested statements:

Cows can type.	Cows eat grass.	Cows have tails.
Cows can talk.	Cows can read.	Cows say, "Moo."
Cows live on farms.	Cows wear clothing.	Cows can dance.

Cut out a class supply of the notes on page 183 and send each one home with youngsters when appropriate. What a simple way to encourage at-home discussion of the book!

Cow Cards

Use with "Would You?" on page 179.

TEC41072

TEC41072

TEC41072

TEC41072

TEC41072

TEC41072

Take-Home Cards

Use with "Cow Craft" on page 179 and as take-home notes for the books on pages 179 through 181.

Today, we read
Kiss the Cow!
Written by Phyllis Root
Illustrated by Will Hillenbrand

Ask me what happened
in the story.

Today, we read
*Click, Clack, Moo:
Cows That Type*
Written by Doreen Cronin
Illustrated by Betsy Lewin

Ask me what happened
in the story.

©The Mailbox® • TEC41072 • April/May 2014

©The Mailbox® • TEC41072 • April/May 2014

Today, we read
Cows Can't Fly
by David Milgrim

Ask me what happened
in the story.

©The Mailbox® • TEC41072 • April/May 2014

Who Sank the Boat?

by Pamela Allen

A cow, a donkey, a sheep, a pig, and a tiny little mouse all get into a rowboat one by one. Each time, the narrator asks if that particular animal sank the boat. In the end, it's the tiny mouse that sends them all into the lake!

Who Will Sink It?

Making predictions, organizing data

Get little ones excited for the story with this activity! Prepare a simple chart like the one shown. (If desired, attach pictures of animals to the chart for visual clues.) Begin reading the book, stopping when you get to the line "Do you know who sank the boat?" Review the animals with youngsters and then ask students to predict the answer to the question. Use tally marks to record students' guesses. Then have youngsters help you count up the tally marks and write each number on the chart. Have students compare the numbers. Then finish reading the story!

cow	donkey	pig	sheep	mouse
~~||||~~	||	||||			
5	2	4	1	0

 Check out page 185 for an **activity page** for your little ones!

Cruiser Capacity

Exploring capacity

Place a clean foam tray (boat) near your water table along with a variety of plastic toy animals. Youngsters place the tray atop the water and then place animals on the tray, counting as they go, to discover how many animals will fit on the tray until it tips or sinks.

Tricia Kylene Brown, Bowling Green, KY

Preschoolers Aboard!

Participating in a group activity

Cut out a full-body photo of each child. Also get a cutout of a mouse. Draw a large boat on a large sheet of paper and display it in your room. Attach a child's photo to the boat and say, "Did [student's name] sink the boat?" Encourage the child to say, "No, I didn't sink the boat!" Continue with each remaining child. Then attach the mouse and say, "Did the mouse sink the boat?" Encourage students to say, "Yes!" Then have them say, "Glub, glub, glub!" as if the boat has sunk. What fun!

Who Sank the Boat?

by Pamela Allen

What happens in the story?

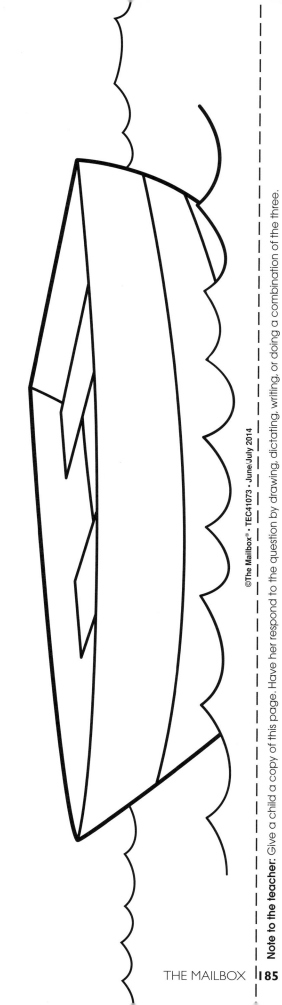

©The Mailbox® • TEC41073 • June/July 2014

Note to the teacher: Give a child a copy of this page. Have her respond to the question by drawing, dictating, writing, or doing a combination of the three.

Storytime at the ZOO

These whimsical and fun storytime options feature two zookeepers and two very unique bunches of animals!

Good Night, Gorilla
by Peggy Rathmann

As a sleepy zookeeper bids the animals good night, a mischievous gorilla frees them and quietly leads them to the zookeeper's home. The zookeeper's startled wife returns all the animals to the zoo—all except the sneaky gorilla and its mouse companion!

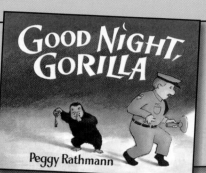

Raise Your G!
Letter-sound association

Before a read-aloud of the story, give each child a letter G card. Tell students that, in the story, a sneaky gorilla lets all the animals out of their cages at the zoo. Have youngsters say the word *gorilla* and listen for the /g/ sound. Say, "When you see the gorilla on a page, hold up your letter G cards." Then read the story aloud.

Tricia Kylene Brown, Bowling Green, KY

Did your little ones see the mouse pulling a banana in the line of animals in this story? For extra storytime fun, attach a string to a plastic banana. When students line up, give it to the child at the end of the line and have him pull the banana as you walk to your destination. Fun!

Add Some Sound!
Participating in an interactive read-aloud

Good Night, Gorilla only has a few words, so youngsters will be excited to add some sound to this rereading! Gather a hand drum (or an empty oatmeal canister) and a key ring with several keys. Read the story, prompting youngsters to make a noise for each animal, such as a roar for the lion, and encouraging a child to jingle the keys whenever the gorilla frees one of its friends. When the line of animals walks out of the zoo and into the house, have a child play the hand drum so it sounds like footsteps. Finally, prompt each student to give a big yawn with the gorilla and repeat the walking noises as the animals go back to the zoo! If desired, place the props at a center along with the book for independent play.

A Sick Day For Amos McGee

Written by Philip C. Stead
Illustrated by Erin E. Stead

Amos McGee works at the zoo. While there, he spends special time with his friends. He plays chess with the elephant, sits with the penguin, takes care of the rhino, and reads to the owl. One day, Amos is sick and stays home. So his friends come to his house and take care of him!

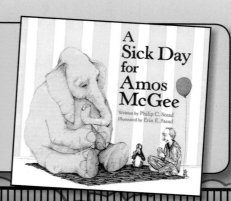

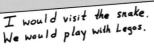

I would visit the snake. We would play with Legos.

Lions
Elephants

Zoo Friends
Creating a story innovation

Review the animals that Amos visited and the activities they did together. Then ask youngsters what animal they would choose to visit at a zoo and what they would want to do with that animal. Write each child's words on a sheet of paper and then have her draw an accompanying picture. Bind the pictures together with a cover labeled "The Preschoolers Always Made Time to Visit Their Zoo Friends!"

Take a Walk
Retelling a story, taking a picture walk

Have little ones use the pictures to tell the story! In advance, get a red bingo dauber. The day after the read-aloud of the book, say, "You may have noticed that many pages in this book have a red balloon." Have little ones help you describe what is happening on each page as you search for the balloon. Each time youngsters see the balloon, have a child make a mark with the bingo dauber on a sheet of chart paper. At the end of the story, add strings to the prints so they resemble balloons. Then help students count them aloud.

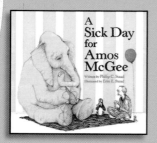

My Favorite!
Expressing an opinion, organizing data

Cut out copies of the animal cards on page 188. Decorate two sheets of construction paper so they resemble zoo gates and then place them on a table. Place *Good Night, Gorilla* near one gate and *A Sick Day for Amos McGee* near the other. Have each child choose an animal card and color it. Then have her think about which book is her favorite and place the animal on the corresponding gate. After each child has had a chance to vote, help students count the animals and compare the results.

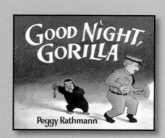

TEC41073

TEC41073

TEC41073

TEC41073

TEC41073

TEC41073

CENTER UNITS

Fabulous Family Centers

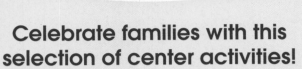

Celebrate families with this selection of center activities!

Parents and Children

Fine-Motor Area

Little ones learn sorting skills as they get a fine-motor workout! Provide magazines, scissors, and two large sheets of paper labeled as shown. Encourage youngsters to cut pictures of people from the magazines and then glue children and parents onto the corresponding sheets. **Sorting**

Abigail's Family

Mom Dad Abigail Jacob Aaron Boots

A Handsome Family!

Art Center

This unique family craft looks adorable displayed in the classroom. Prompt a child to brush colorful paint onto a sheet of paper as desired. Help her fold down the fingers on hand die-cuts to show the number of people (and pets, if desired) in her family. Have her glue the hands to the paper. When the paint is dry, have her dictate the names of her family members as you write them above the fingers. Label the craft as shown. **Identifying members of one's family**

Tricia Kylene Brown, Bowling Green, KY

Baby Moves!

Gross-Motor Area

Many of your youngsters may have babies in their families! Create a simple obstacle course and place a rattle at the end of the course. Encourage youngsters to pretend they are babies and crawl through the course, grab the rattle, and then crawl back. The child places the rattle back in its original location for the next child. *Developing gross-motor skills*

Roxanne LaBell Dearman
NC Early Intervention Program for Children Who Are Deaf or Hard of Hearing
Charlotte, NC

Bear Families

Math Center

Cut out a copy of the cards on page 192 and place them at a center along with bear counters. A child chooses a card and counts the bears on it. Then he makes an identical family of bears with the counters. *Counting, creating sets*

 No bear counters? Use large and small pom-poms to represent bear families.

Family Talk

Literacy Center

Have each child bring in a photo of her family. Lightly attach the photos to a tabletop and then place a clear Plexiglas sheet over the photos. (Plexiglas sheets are available at your local home improvement store.) As an alternative to a Plexiglas sheet, place a piece of lamination film over the photos and tape it to the tabletop. Encourage youngsters to look at the family photos and discuss what they see. *Speaking*

Angela Arndt
Sicklerville, NJ

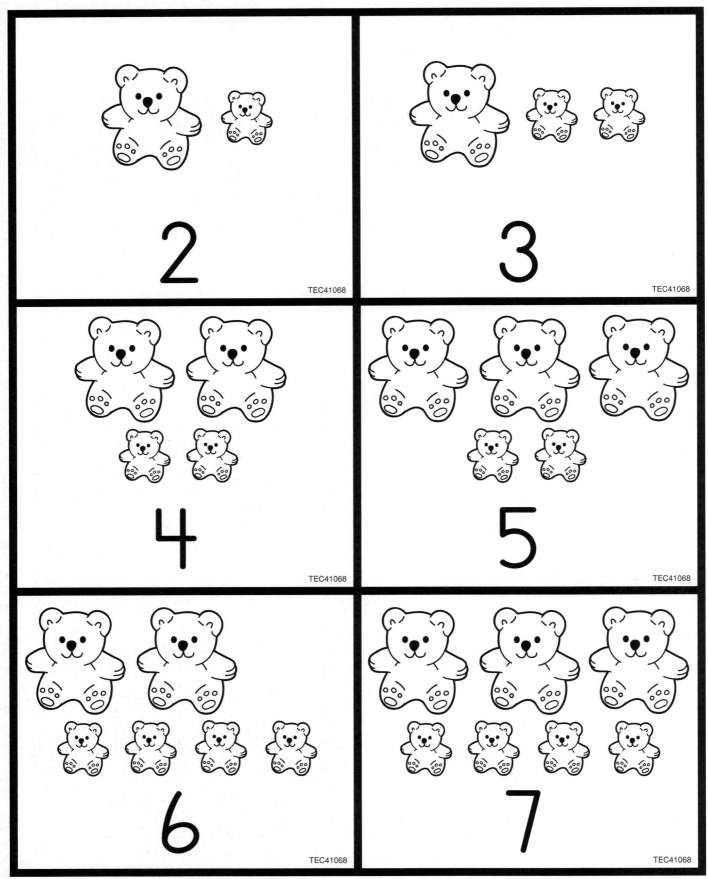

TEC41068

TEC41068

TEC41068

TEC41068

TEC41068

TEC41068

Sticky Centers

What do all of these centers have in common? Why, sticky stuff, of course!

ideas contributed by Ada Goren, Winston-Salem, NC

● Tape and Dot Letters
Literacy Center

Help youngsters notice that there are straight lines and curved lines in letters with this sticky solution! Write letters with both straight and curved lines on sheets of paper and place the papers at your center along with colored masking tape and sticky dots. A child visits the center and chooses a letter. He identifies the letter, with help as needed. Then he traces it with his finger, noticing that there are straight lines and curved lines. He attaches masking tape to the straight lines and sticky dots to the curved lines! *Forming letters, identifying letters*

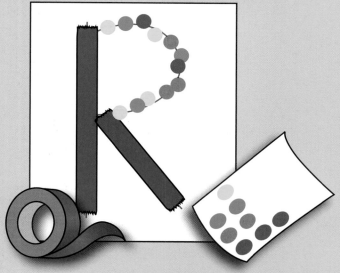

● Which Glue Will Do?
Science Center

Youngsters take part in product evaluation at this center! Provide glue sticks, white school glue, and tacky craft glue. Also provide sheets of construction paper and a variety of items to be glued down, such as tissue paper, scrapbook paper, aluminum foil scraps, pieces of pipe cleaner, and craft feathers. Make a chart similar to the one shown. A child uses the different adhesives to attach items to a sheet of paper, evaluating how well the adhesives work with the different items. When she is finished gluing, she writes her name beneath her preferred adhesive. (Discuss the results of the chart during group time.) *Observing and evaluating, expressing an opinion*

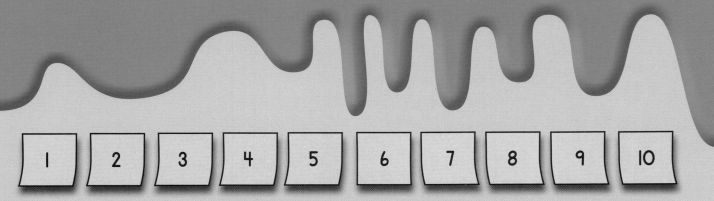

Peel and Position
Math Center

Write the numbers one to ten on individual sticky notes. (Depending on your youngsters' abilities, you may want to include numbers 11–20 as well.) Randomly stick the notes to a tabletop. If desired, provide a number line for reference. A child peels the notes and repositions them in order. *Ordering numbers*

Double-Stick Art
Art Center

This abstract process art will look sensational displayed in your classroom! To make one, a child attaches double-stick tape to a sheet of colorful construction paper. Then she presses small pieces of tissue paper, aluminum foil, and scrapbook paper to the tape. Lovely! *Fine-motor skills*

Stick It On!
Block Center

Attach the hook sides of Velcro fasteners to random blocks in your block center. Provide colorful pom-poms. Youngsters visit the center and build with the blocks. Then they stick pom-poms to the Velcro fasteners. These block constructions look like artsy sculptures! *Spatial skills*

A Sticky Tip!

When little ones are chatty during circle time, Kimberly Russo from First Steps Child Care Center in Danvers, Massachusetts, gives each child an index card. Then she tells youngsters to blow their "sticky words" on the card to save for later. After circle time, students can "peel" their words off their cards to share them. What a cute and whimsical tip!

It's Not Just for Pancakes!
Writing Center

This simple center is sticky and tasty! Tape a disposable plate to a tabletop. Drizzle maple syrup (or tinted light corn syrup) on the plate. A child uses his pointer finger to draw lines, shapes, and letters in the syrup. *Forming letters*

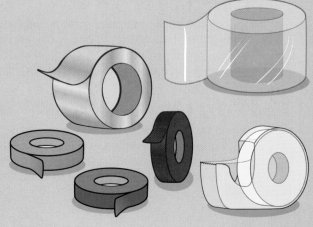

Pick, Pick, Pick
Fine-Motor Area

Do you have little ones with restless fingers? Send them to this center! Attach a wide variety of stickers to a sheet of poster board and then place the poster board at a center. A youngster sits and picks at the stickers, eventually removing them from the board. This process is excellent fine-motor practice, and it's soothing! *Fine-motor skills*

Totally Tape!
Discovery Center

Encourage youngsters to investigate different types of tape at this center. Provide masking tape, invisible tape, electrical tape, packing tape, and duct tape. Also provide scissors. Attach a sheet of paper to the table. Youngsters remove pieces of tape and compare their stickiness. When they are finished exploring, they attach the pieces of tape to the paper. After everyone has had a chance to explore, hang the resulting tape mural in the classroom. *Comparing to form a conclusion*

Center Time

With Puppet Pals!

Incorporate puppets into your centers to encourage speaking, teamwork, and educational fun!

Dramatic-Play Area

- Cut out a copy of the emotion cards on page 197 and put them in the center along with two puppets. Each of two youngsters dons a puppet and chooses a card. The pair identifies the emotion. Then the puppets have a conversation involving the chosen emotion! *Identifying emotions*

Literacy Center

- Provide familiar picture books and puppets. A student chooses a picture book and puts on a puppet. Then she uses the puppet to tell the story or discuss the pictures. *Telling a story, developing book awareness*

Art Center

- Place sock puppets at your art center along with paints and paper. A child attaches a sheet of paper to the easel, slides a puppet onto her dominant hand, and picks up a paintbrush. Then she has her puppet paint a fantastic masterpiece! *Expressing oneself through art*

Music Center

- Provide puppets, recordings of familiar songs, and simple rhythm instruments. Youngsters can don puppets and have the puppets pick up instruments (with their mouths, of course). Then the puppets can have a jam session. Or students can play the musical recording and the puppets can "sing along" with the words. *Developing musical expression*

Fine-Motor Area

- Place craft sticks at a center along with a variety of craft items, such as scrap paper, pom-poms, craft foam shapes, yarn, and tissue paper. Youngsters make their own critters with the supplies, use tape to attach craft sticks, and then have their very own puppet shows with their stick puppets! *Fine-motor skills*

Math Center

- Place two puppets and a bowl of small pom-poms at the center. Each of two students puts on a puppet and then each puppet uses its mouth to scoop up a bunch of pom-poms! Each puppet makes an enthusiastic "pitooey!" noise as it spits out its pom-poms. Then each child counts his set and compares it to his classmate's set. *Counting, comparing sets*

happy

TEC41070

sad

TEC41070

angry

TEC41070

excited

TEC41070

Switch-Out Centers

You know when you go to the frozen yogurt shop and you have an endless choice of add-ins? Well, this is kind of like that—only with centers. Choose an item (or items) to add to a center and watch little ones get creative. When interest wanes, choose a different add-in.

Play Dough Center

Try one of these center add-ins for some fun and unique play dough exploration! *Suzanne Moore, Tucson, AZ*

- potato mashers
- cupcake liners
- milk jug caps
- plastic leaves
- craft sticks
- chenille stems
- pots and pans
- marker caps
- drinking straws

Block Center

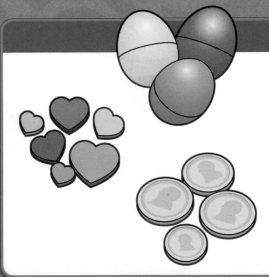

Rotate these seasonal items in your center to add to little ones' building experiences. *Janet Boyce, Cokato, MN*

- September: plastic apples
- October: pictures of jack-o'-lanterns and black craft foam shapes
- November: gourds
- December: green and red ribbon and scissors
- January: cotton batting
- February: craft foam hearts
- March: green pom-poms and large play coins
- April: plastic eggs
- May: plastic insects
- June: plastic picnic cups and plates

Literacy Center

Here are some exciting and engaging options!
- sets of paper plates labeled with matching letters (or uppercase and lowercase letters)
- letter cards and self-adhesive craft foam shapes
- soda bottles and coordinating bottle caps labeled with letters
- sticky notes labeled with letters
- letter pointers and big books
- smooth rocks labeled with letters
- letter cards (only letters with straight lines) and craft sticks
- magazines and highlighters

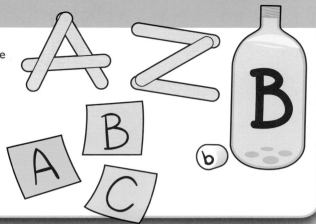

Fine-Motor Area

Place tongs or tweezers at the center along with empty containers and one (or two) of the following items:
- colorful pom-poms
- dyed pasta
- linking cubes
- plastic animals
- plastic egg halves
- cardboard tubes cut into rings
- plastic utensils
- paper shreds
- puzzle pieces
- sponges cut into pieces

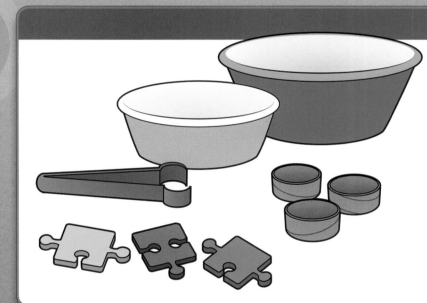

Math Center

Provide these items and watch little ones explore math concepts.
- number cards and rounded-end toothpicks
- paper plates and bear counters
- colorful craft sticks with magnets attached to the ends and a cookie sheet
- large dice and wooden blocks
- toy vehicles and number cards
- play dough and shape cards
- squares of colorful construction paper and matching linking cubes
- hoops and multiple sets of number cards
- self-adhesive craft foam shapes and strips of paper

Time to Plant!

Garden Centers

Water the Plants
Fine-Motor Area

Fine-motor skills will grow with this adorable center! Get a watering can that has several holes and place it at a center along with white or silver pipe cleaners. A youngster pushes the pipe cleaners into the holes of the watering can so it looks like water is streaming out. Then she pretends to water a garden! *Developing fine-motor skills, investigating the needs of living things*

Janet Boyce
Cokato, MN

Row by Row
Writing Center

Spread potting soil in a shallow tray and provide dots hole-punched from craft foam (seeds). A child uses his finger to draw several straight lines in the soil so they resemble garden rows. Then he places seeds in each row and carefully covers them up. **For a more challenging version,** provide seed packets. A child chooses a packet and looks at the name of the seeds. Then he uses his finger to form letters from the name in the soil. *Developing writing skills, forming letters*

Sprout!
Science Center

This simple, quick growing experiment is easy to prepare. Get radish or alfalfa seeds and several sponges. Cut the sponges into small rectangles. Have each child soak a piece of sponge in water and then wring most of the water out. Next, have him place the sponge on a small plastic plate. Then prompt him to sprinkle seeds on the wet sponge. Seal each plate in a resealable plastic bag and then place it by a window. Youngsters will love to examine the sprouting seeds with a magnifying glass. *Investigating living things*

Darlene Taig, Willow Creek Preschool, Westland, MI

This investigation also works well with grass seed. When the grass gets tall enough, youngsters can cut it with scissors.

Weed Whacking
Literacy Center

Is it a weed, or is it a plant? Sometimes it's difficult to tell! Make several copies of the weed and plant cards on page 202, cut them out, and place them facedown on a length of brown bulletin board paper (garden). Two youngsters visit the center. Each child, in turn, flips a card. If the card has a W, it's a weed; the child whacks it with her hand and then removes it from the garden. If it isn't a weed, the child leaves the plant in the garden. The students continue until all the weeds have been removed.

adapted from an idea by Tricia Kylene Brown, Bowling Green, KY

Seed Match
Math Center

Number raindrop cutouts from 1 to 10 (or higher to make this center more challenging) and place them in a watering can. Draw ten seed cutouts on a strip of paper and number them as shown. A child removes a raindrop from the watering can, names the number, and then places it on the matching number on the seed strip. She continues with each remaining raindrop.

Tricia Kylene Brown

| 1 | 2 | 3 | 4 | 5 | 6 | 7 | 8 | 9 | 10 |

Weed and Plant Cards

Use with "Weed Whacking" on page 201.

TEC41072

TEC41072

TEC41072

TEC41072

TEC41072

TEC41072

U.P, UP, AND AWAY!

Superhero Centers

ideas contributed by Ada Goren
Lewisville, NC

Look the Part!
Dramatic-Play Area

Encourage imaginative play with a wealth of superhero gear! Gather towels or small blankets (capes) and binder clips or hair clips to hold them in place, simple masks, colorful gloves, tool belts, strips of fabric (headbands), and belts. Make simple cardboard shields and hot-glue a strip of fabric to the back of each one to make a handle. To make wrist cuffs, cut sections of cardboard tubes, as shown, and encourage students to paint them bright colors. Place all the items at a center to encourage superhero scenarios!

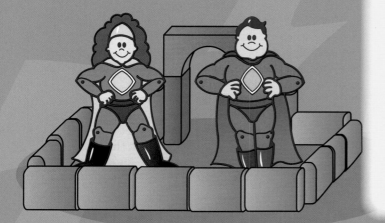

Good-Guy Headquarters
Block Center

Villains may have their lairs, but superheroes need headquarters! Place superhero toy figures and toy cars in your block center and then invite your little builders to create a secure facility for the superheroes. Encourage little ones to build a control room where calls for help can be received; a garage where the supervehicles can be parked, and items to promote security, such as a fence or a moat.

Lin is a super artist!

That's Super!
Literacy Center

Gather two or three youngsters for this center. Explain to the students that superheroes have superpowers, such as flying, being really strong, or being invisible. But everyone is super at something! Give each child a simple shield cutout with a large *S* on it. Have her name the letter and its sound and then say the word *super*, listening for /s/. Next, have her name something she is super at doing. Write the words on her shield in the format shown. Then use a safety pin to attach her shield to her shirt.

Kim Harker, Discovery Express Preschool, Mendon, UT

Time to Fly
Art Center

To prepare, have each child wear a small towel or blanket so it resembles a superhero cape. (A binder clip or hair clip is useful for holding it in place.) Then have her lie on the floor in a position that mimics flying. Take a photo of the youngster and print it. Then help the child cut out the photo and glue it to a sheet of paper so she appears to be flying. Next, encourage her to add details below her photo. Is she flying over tall buildings? A farm? A forest? She may want to add details—such as an airplane, a sun, or clouds—in the air on her artwork as well.

Save the People!
Math Center

This active center is sure to be popular with your little superheroes! Place number cards in a bag and gather a supply of people cutouts. Scatter the people on the floor and place the bag several feet away. If desired, provide a cape as described in "Time to Fly" (above). A little superhero wears his cape and chooses a number. He identifies the number. Then he says, "Up, up, and away!" and "flies" to save the people! He picks up the correct number of people and "flies" back. Then he places the people on the floor and says, "You're safe now!" He repeats the process until all the people have been saved. Now that's a successful superhero!

LITERACY UNITS

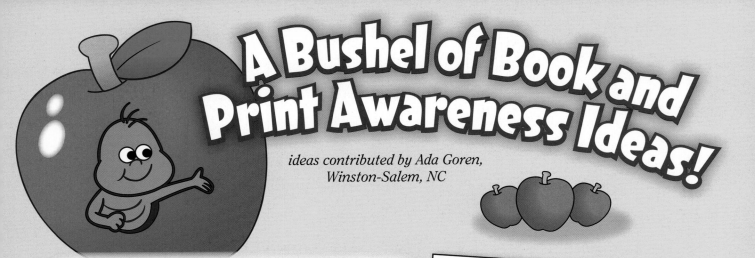

A Bushel of Book and Print Awareness Ideas!

ideas contributed by Ada Goren,
Winston-Salem, NC

Environmental Expedition
Recognizing environmental print

Grab a notepad and pen and take little ones on a print walk! Lead youngsters around the classroom, through hallways, and outdoors in search of environmental print, like posters, flyers, and labels as well as exit, bathroom, and handicap signs. Jot down the examples and then write them on chart paper when the expedition is over. Review the list of environmental print with students; then encourage them to be on the lookout for more print to add to the list.

Environmental Print

boys' and girls' bathroom signs

exit sign

elevator sign

fire extinguisher sign

bus stop sign

library poster

Left to Right

I go from left to right.

I go from left to right.

I know which way to go

When I read and I write!

Perfect Progression
Tracking print from left to right and top to bottom

Write the song shown on chart paper and make a simple worm pointer. Tell little ones you're going to teach them a new song but you want to sing it to them first. Then place the worm at the bottom right of the song and sing each line backward, moving the worm from right to left and bottom to top as you sing. You're sure to get peculiar looks and giggles! Say, "Oh my, that didn't sound right! I followed this little worm, and it was going in the wrong direction!" Then place the worm at the correct starting point and lead youngsters in singing the song the correct way.

(sung to the tune of "The Farmer in the Dell")

I go from left to right.
I go from left to right.
I know which way to go
When I read and I write!

song contributed by Roxanne LaBell Dearman
NC Early Intervention Program for Children Who Are Deaf or
    Hard of Hearing
Charlotte, NC

I Write, You Draw
Understanding the roles of author and illustrator

Open a picture book and draw youngsters' attention to the text and illustrations. Explain that the author writes the words and the illustrator draws the pictures. Then pretend to be the author and elicit the help of a volunteer to be the illustrator. Write a simple sentence on a wipe-off board. Then have the illustrator draw a picture that illustrates the sentence. Continue with other simple sentences (see the suggestions shown) and volunteer illustrators.

Sentence suggestions: *I see a ball. The sun is out. The worm is brown. The banana is yellow.*

Point It Out
Identifying parts of a book

Examine a book with youngsters and discuss some of its elements, such as the *front,* the *back,* the *top,* and the *bottom* of the book. Next, give each child a book to hold. Then sing the song shown, prompting youngsters to point to the *front* of the book. Continue in the same way with the remaining verses.

(sung to the tune of "London Bridge")

Where is the [front] of your book?
Point it out on your book.
Where is the [front] of your book,
My young readers?

Continue with the following: *back, top, bottom*

I Love Apples!
Understanding that words are separated by spaces

Gather a small group of children and give each child a copy of page 208. Explain that words are groups of letters and there are spaces between the words. Then read the poem aloud, pointing to each word as you read. Have each child point to several spaces she sees between the words of the poem. Next, encourage each child to make a red fingerprint (apple) in each space. If desired, help each child use fine-tip markers to add details to each apple.

 # I Love Apples!

Apples   are   big.

Apples   are   small.

I   love   apples.

I'll   eat   them   all!

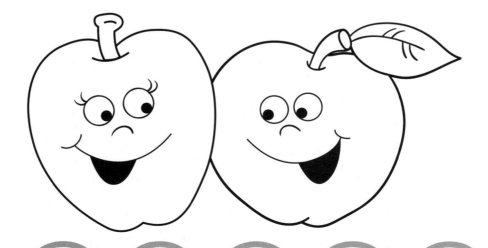

Note to the teacher: Use with "I Love Apples!" on page 207.

Word play!

You'll get lots of giggles with these fun phonological awareness activities!

Silly Word Jump!

Youngsters manipulate phonemes and develop gross-motor skills! In advance, make three or four supersize consonant letter cutouts and attach them to your floor with Con-Tact covering. To begin, review the sounds of the chosen letters. Then call out a word, such as *rattle*. Have a child jump on each letter. As he does so, he substitutes the first letter in *rattle* with the sound of the letter he's jumping on (with help as needed). So he might say, "Mattle, lattle, sattle!" Continue with each youngster. Keep the letters attached to your floor and choose a new word each day.

B. Martin, Nora Stewart Early Learning Center
Columbia, MO

Hey! What else can I do with these letter cards?

- During center time, provide manipulatives with names that begin with the letters, such as a tub of pasta for the letter *P* or rocks for the letter *R*. A child places manipulatives along each letter.

- Provide beanbags. A child tosses a beanbag toward the letters and then names the letter it lands on.

- Place letter cards in a bag, including the letters that are on the floor. A child draws a card and names the letter, with help as needed. If it's one of the letters on the floor, he stomps on the appropriate letter.

Song Play

Tweak favorite songs for a unique musical experience! Choose a common song, such as "The Muffin Man." Lead students in singing the song. Then say, "Let's change the words 'Muffin Man' so they begin with /t/ instead of /m/." Have students help you sing, "Do you know the Tuffin Tan?" Then repeat the process with a new sound!

Lisa Kerr, St. Lucas Preschool, Bay View, WI

Apple, Bapple, Tapple

Rhyming nonsense words are the focus of this little song! Gather a few simple objects, such as an apple, a pencil, and scissors. Have a student choose an object. Then help youngsters name two nonsense words that rhyme with the object's name. Next, guide them in singing the song, inserting the object name and nonsense words as shown. Continue with other objects.

(sung to the tune of "The Farmer in the Dell")

[Apple, bapple, tapple],
[Apple, bapple, tapple],
Silly song—let's sing along!
[Apple, bapple, tapple].

Jenny

Brooks

Name Game

To begin, chant, "Who wants to play the name game?" Encourage students to chant back, "We want to play the name game!" Then write a child's name on the board incorrectly. For example, write "Sate" for "Kate." Allow a moment for youngsters to giggle at your mistake. Then help students figure out the name of the child and have the child help you correct it, with help as needed.

Heather Cash, St. Edward School, Appleton, WI

Albert

Emma

Later!

Youngsters will soon join in chanting this engaging dismissal rhyme! Cut out a copy of the cards on page 211 and ready them for flannelboard use. Then lead youngsters in reciting the chant shown, placing each appropriate card on your flannelboard.

See you later, alligator.
Give a hug, ladybug.
Be sweet, parakeet.
Take care, polar bear.
So long, King Kong.
Out the door, dinosaur.
Gotta fly, pizza pie!

Karen Engram, Selma F. Bartlett Elementary, Henderson, NV

TEC41070

TEC41070

TEC41070

TEC41070

TEC41070

TEC41070

TEC41070

Learning Letters and Sounds!

Cap the Jug!
Letter-sound association

This literacy activity also develops fine-motor skills! Gather several clean, small plastic milk jugs. Remove the caps and write a different letter on each cap. On each jug, draw a simple picture (or attach a picture) of an item that begins with one of the letters. Place the jugs and caps at a center. Then have youngsters screw (or snap) the caps onto the matching jugs.

Karen Eiben
The Learning House Preschool
LaSalle, IL

Windy Day
Recognizing letters

Draw three or four letters on your board. Then give each child a cotton ball (cloud). Say, "The wind blew away the [letter name]!" Have a child find the appropriate letter and erase it with his cloud while making dramatic wind sound effects. Continue until all the letters have been blown away. Then write a new set of letters on the board!

Rexann Roussel
Narrow Acres Preschool
Paulina, LA

To **practice letter sounds** with this activity, say the sound of the letter instead of its name!

Find a Letter!
Matching letters

Print out a simple word search puzzle (an Internet search will turn up plenty of child-friendly options). Then make multiple copies of the puzzle and place it at a center along with colorful highlighters, a magnifying glass, and letter cards that correspond to letters in the word search. A child takes a word search. Then she chooses a card and uses a highlighter to mark that letter wherever it occurs on the puzzle. For added fun, she uses the magnifying glass to assist her in her search!

Litsa Jackson
Covington Integrated Arts Academy
Covington, TN

Learning the Letter *R*
Identifying letters

This adorable song will help little ones remember the letter *R*. Give each child a sheet of paper labeled with the letter *R*. Then lead youngsters in singing the song and hopping their fingers along the letter as described in the lyrics.

(sung to the tune of "The Bear Went Over the Mountain")

The rabbit went up the mountain.
The rabbit went round the mountain.
The rabbit went down the mountain
To make the letter *R*.

Jodi Norton
Next Step Christian Childcare and Preschool
Burlington, IA

LMNO Peas
by Keith Baker
Letter-sound association

Read aloud *LMNO Peas* by Keith Baker. In this book, happy little pea characters with a variety of personalities and careers cavort about brightly colored letters. Next, give each child a copy of page 215 and a green pom-pom (pea). Say, "/w/, /w/, /w/!" Then encourage little ones to find the letter that makes that sound and have each child hop his pea up and down on the letter. Continue with other letter sounds.

Janice Johnston, Growing Tree Preschool, Chambersburg, PA

Looking for extra fun with peas? Have students use green bingo daubers to make peas on a bubble letter. Then draw a face on each pea!

A Song About Sounds
Letter-sound association

Here's a simple song and activity to help little ones recall letter sounds. Gather the following letter cards: *B, S, D, T, M,* and *P.* Then hold up the letter *B* and lead students in singing the song. Repeat the process for each remaining letter card, altering the words as indicated below.

(sung to the tune of "Bingo")

Oh, won't you sing a song with me—a song about a [*B*]?
Bug, bat, basketball,
Bug, bat, basketball,
Bug, bat, basketball,
Yes, that's the letter [*B*]!

Continue with the following:
S; saw, seal, sunflower
D; dog, dish, dinosaur
T; tub, tie, telephone
M; mud, map, manatee
P; pig, pie, parachute

Faith Hann
Harmony Township School
Phillipsburg, NJ

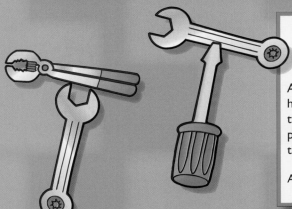

Tool Ts
Forming letters

Little ones will be eager to visit this center to make unique letter *Ts.* Attach a length of bulletin board paper to a table and provide a variety of hand tools, such as screwdrivers, wrenches, and pliers. A child chooses two different tools and explores them. Then she arranges them on the paper to form a letter *T.* Next, she traces around the tools and colors in the tracing as desired. Youngsters continue adding *Ts* to the paper.

Aline Dyson, Ripley Primary School, Ripley, TN

Human Pencils
Forming letters

Forming letters with this active method gives little ones important practice crossing the midline! When learning or reviewing a letter, have little ones stand. Then tell them that they are going to pretend to be giant pencils. Prompt them to point their dominant hand straight up so it resembles the lead of the pencil. Then have them move their bodies to form a letter. For example, to form a letter *V,* a child would begin with his pencil lead pointing to the upper left. Then he would move the lead at an angle all the way to the floor and then at an angle to the upper right.

Mary Ellen Moore, Miller Elementary, Canton, MI

Find the Letters!

C	F	W
L	Z	H

Write On!

Writing skills are sure to bloom with this collection of spring-themed activities!

Writers in Bloom

Dictating information to be written down

Give each child in a small group a coffee filter and a paper circle programmed with the sentence starter shown. Encourage him to draw designs on the filter using colorful washable markers. Then have him spritz the filter with water to blend the colors. While the filter is drying, read the sentence starter aloud and have him dictate words for you to write to complete the sentence. Then have him glue the circle to the center of the filter and add a paper stem and leaves. If desired, display the resulting flowers on a spring-themed board with the title "Writers in Bloom!"

What I like best about spring is...
splashing in puddles!

Jake

Mighty Mud

Developing writing skills, forming letters

Little ones won't hear "Stay out of the mud!" with this fun activity. Spread a thick layer of mud (or brown fingerpaint mixed with oatmeal) in a shallow tray and place it at a table. Stack facedown near the tray several cards programmed with letters, numbers, or shapes. Provide tools for writing, such as a twig, an unsharpened pencil, a craft stick, and a wood dowel. Invite a child to flip a card. Then encourage her to choose a writing tool and copy the item from the card in the mud. When she's finished, have her "erase" her work with the back of a spoon and then flip another card.

Elizabeth Cook
St. Louis, MO

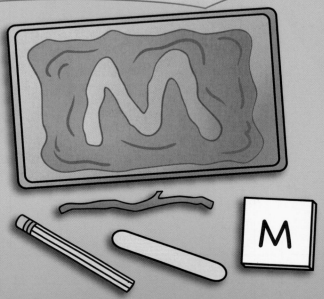

Rainy-Day Rebus

Developing print concepts, dictating information to be written down

Inspire your preschoolers to create a rainy-day rebus story! Prepare rain-related cutouts such as a raindrop, a puddle, an umbrella, and rain boots. Also make a gray cloud cutout. Put all the cutouts except the cloud in a bag. Write on chart paper "One spring day, I looked out the window and saw a big gray _____ in the sky." Lightly attach the cloud to the blank space. To begin, read the sentence aloud, pausing and prompting students to say the word *cloud*. Then randomly take a cutout from the bag and have students identify it. Encourage youngsters to add to the story, incorporating the cutout as a story detail. Write on the chart paper as they dictate their words, inserting the cutout in place of the written word. Continue with the remaining cutouts to complete the story.

One Spring Day

One spring day, I looked out the window and saw a big gray ☁ in the sky. Then I saw a 💧 hit the window.

Absolutely Adorable!

Dictating information to be written down

What's cuter than animals born in the springtime? The sounds they make! Make a supply of speech bubble cutouts. Encourage a child to draw a baby animal on a sheet of paper. Help the child say the specific baby animal name. Then ask her what noise the animal makes. Write the words on a speech bubble. Then have her attach the speech bubble to her page.

Elizabeth Cook, St. Louis, MO

Simple Scenes

Invented writing

Place spring-themed magazines or catalogs at a center. Provide scissors, paper, markers, and glue. Invite several children to the center. Help each child look through the literature and cut or tear out a picture that depicts some type of action, emotion, or event. Have him glue the picture to a sheet of paper and then study the details more closely. Then encourage him to "write" on his page to tell about the picture.

Latoya Johnson, Baytown, TX

Sand, Sun, and Fun!

Beach-Time Literacy

B Is for *Beach*

Letter-sound association, beginning sounds, letter formation

Give each child a sheet of construction paper labeled with the letter *B*. Have her trace the letter with a finger and say its name and sound. Say, "*Beach* begins with /b/. Let's make our letter *B* into a beach!" Have her brush glue on the paper and then sprinkle a mixture of sand and glitter on the glue. Next, have her glue dyed mini pasta shells to the letter. Each time she glues one down, encourage her to say, "/b/, beach."

Sue Fleischmann
Sussex, WI

Feeling Crabby?

Dictating information to be written down, writing

Give each child a copy of page 220 and have her place the lower half of the paper over a piece of sandpaper. Have her rub the side of an unwrapped crayon over the paper to make a beach-like texture. Next, have her attach a red circle cutout (crab body) to the beach and red paper strips (legs and eye stalks) to the body. Finally, have her glue semicircle cutouts (claws) and eye cutouts to complete the crab. Tell her that people often say that they're feeling crabby when they're in a bad mood. Ask, "What makes you crabby?" Then write her words (or have her "write" her own words) where indicated.

Beach Day
Developing rhyming skills

In advance, get a beach toy, such as a beach ball, a plastic sea star, or a small inflatable float. Read aloud *Beach Day* by Karen Roosa. In this rhyming story, families experience a day filled with sand, sun, and sea at the beach. After the read-aloud, randomly turn to a spread of two pages and read the words. Have children notice that there are three rhyming words in the text, such as *boat, float,* and *moat* or *flurry, scurry,* and *hurry*. Next, give the toy to a child and have him name another word (real or nonsense) that rhymes with the three on the page. Continue for another turn and then choose another page!

Whoosh!
Reinforcing letter names

Here's a song that gets little wiggle worms up and moving! Write "WAVES" on your board. Then lead youngsters in performing the song shown. Have a child erase the letter W. Then lead students in performing the song a second time, prompting them to replace the W with "Whoosh!" while they swing their arms so their arms resemble a retreating wave. Continue in the same way for four more verses until all the letters are erased and students say "Whoosh!" five times.

(sung to the tune of "Bingo")

Oh, when I walk along the beach,	*Walk in place.*
The waves go in and out.	*Sway back and forth.*
W-A-V-E-S,	
W-A-V-E-S,	
W-A-V-E-S;	
The waves go in and out.	*Sway back and forth.*

Tricia Kylene Brown, Bowling Green, KY

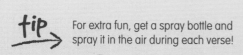

tip → For extra fun, get a spray bottle and spray it in the air during each verse!

Letter Press
Identifying letters, becoming familiar with letter forms

Moisten the sand in your sand table or place moist sand in a tub. Gather letter cookie cutters (or other letter-shaped manipulatives) and place them nearby. A child chooses a letter, identifies it, and then presses it into the sand. He removes it to see the shape of the letter. For extra fun, he uses the manipulatives to spell his name in the sand!

Tricia Kylene Brown

I feel crabby when...

Note to the teacher: Use with "Feeling Crabby?" on page 218.

MATH UNITS

RED, YELLOW, BLUE—
COLOR IDEAS FOR YOU!

YARN WEAVE

Here's a fun way to start off each day of your color unit! Prior to students' arrival, obtain a skein of yarn in your focus color for the day and weave a small portion around the room. When each child arrives, she ducks and steps over the yarn to begin her morning routine. Repeat the activity with each focus color. You're sure to see lots of smiles with this activity!

Becky Ford
Growing Tree Preschool
Chambersburg, PA

SING A SONG OF COLORS

Reinforce color recognition with this catchy tune. For each color, attach a corresponding die-cut shape to a large craft stick. Consider using a red ladybug, a bluebird, a yellow sun, an orange pumpkin, a green frog, a purple butterfly, a brown bear, and a black dog. Distribute the props and invite each youngster who has a prop to stand in front of the class. In turn, have each student hold up his prop as you lead the group in singing the song shown substituting the underlined words as needed.

(sung to the tune of "The Farmer in the Dell")

The [ladybug is red].
The [ladybug is red].
Hold up the [ladybug].
The [ladybug is red].

adapted from an idea by Debbie Feuerstein
New Vernon Presbyterian Nursery School
New Vernon, NJ

BIRDS OF EVERY COLOR

Classroom visitors are sure to smile when they see a display of these quirky and colorful birds! Provide markers, tissue paper squares, and craft feathers in several different colors. Have a child look at the colors and choose his favorite. Next, have him use the marker to draw a circle on a sheet of paper. Direct him to brush glue in the circle and then press tissue paper squares on the glue. Then have him glue feathers to the project. Have him add eye, beak, and leg cutouts. Then encourage him to identify the color. Caption the project as shown.

Joan Schmittel, Warrenton, MO

Blue Bird

SHAKE IT UP

Remove the label from several empty plastic soda bottles. Put water in each bottle until it is about half full and add three tablespoons of dish detergent. Then add four tablespoons of tempera paint to each bottle. Secure the lid and shake. Place the bottles in your discovery area. A child chooses a bottle, names the color of the water, and then shakes the bottle to make colorful suds.

Nardine Rene, Arsingchild Academy, Miami, FL

MY COLOR BOOK

Youngsters use process art to create these one-of-a-kind color books! For each focus color, choose a process art activity (see the suggestions given). Each day, have a child complete the art project. After the projects are dry, have him decorate a front and back cover for his book. Then bind the child's projects between the two covers.

Trisha Cooper, Trisha's Preschool, Spanish Fork, UT

Red: painting with feathers
Blue: crayon rubbing over plastic canvas
Yellow: making prints with crumpled bags
Green: Bubble Wrap cushioning material prints
Purple: paper collage
Orange: painting with kitchen scrubbies

MIX IT!

For each child, divide a paper into four sections. Make a class supply of the color poem on page 225. Gather a few youngsters and give each child a paper. Then squirt a small amount of red paint and blue paint in the upper left quadrant of each child's paper. Have students identify each color and then blend them together with a brush. Continue in the same way with the combinations mentioned in the poem until each quadrant is painted. Then attach the poem to the middle of the paper.

Emily Heffington, Spring Meadows Academy, Spring Hill, TN

Red and blue make purple.
Yellow and blue make green.
Such a lot of colors
To paint a lovely scene!
Red and yellow make orange.
Black and white make gray.
Now I'll dry my brushes
Until another day.

PRIMARY COLORS!

After a color-mixing activity, explain to youngsters that colors they use for mixing—red, blue, and yellow—are called primary colors. Then lead students in performing this action song. When the song is finished, have each standing youngster identify which primary color(s) he's wearing.

(sung to the tune of "If You're Happy and You Know It")

If you're wearing a primary color, please stand up!
If you're wearing a primary color, please stand up!
Every gal and every fellow
Wearing red or blue or yellow—
If you're wearing a primary color, please stand up!

Charlene Stull, St. Mark's Preschool, Waterford, PA

LISTEN AND DRAW

Reinforce your little artists' color-identification skills! Give each child a sheet of drawing paper and access to crayons. Name a color. Encourage the child to choose the crayon color named and then draw on her paper. After several moments, name a different color. Have the child choose the new crayon and continue drawing. Continue in this manner with the remaining colors.

Trudy Van Knowe, Jupiter Academy, Jupiter, FL

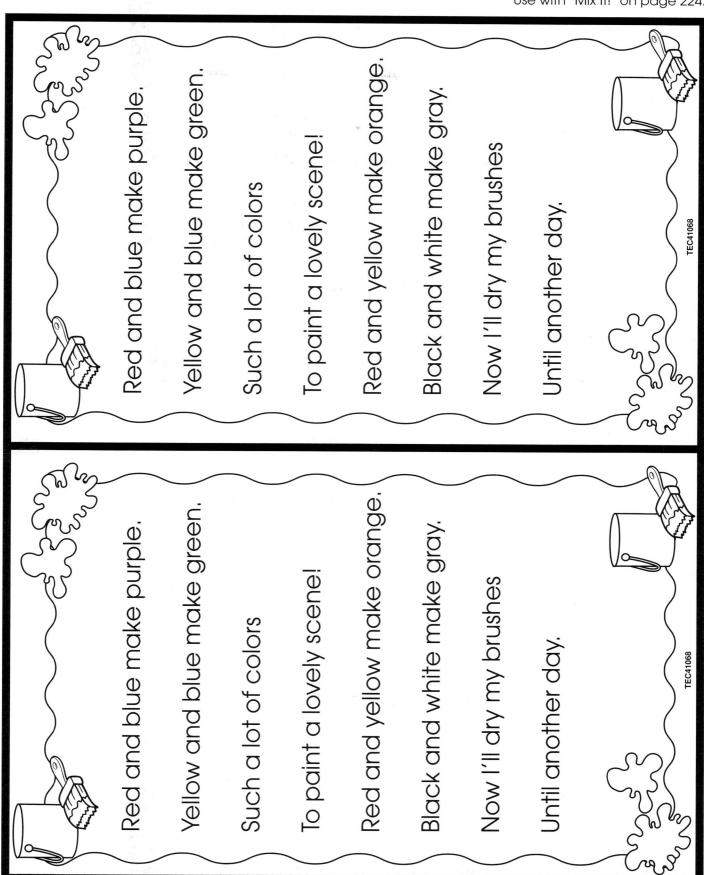

Red and blue make purple.

Yellow and blue make green.

Such a lot of colors

To paint a lovely scene!

Red and yellow make orange.

Black and white make gray.

Now I'll dry my brushes

Until another day.

TEC41068

Red and blue make purple.

Yellow and blue make green.

Such a lot of colors

To paint a lovely scene!

Red and yellow make orange.

Black and white make gray.

Now I'll dry my brushes

Until another day.

TEC41068

Counting

with

Common Manipulatives

Popsicle sticks, linking cubes, stickers—here are some uncommon ideas for using common manipulatives!

Stick and Guess!

Estimating

Give each child a sheet of paper labeled as shown. Then have her attach stickers to the page. Next, have her guess how many stickers are on her page. Help her write the number where indicated. Then encourage her to count the number of stickers, touching each sticker as she counts. Help her write the actual number of stickers below her estimate. Then have her compare the numbers.

Bernie Giordano
Knox Playschool
Redwood City, CA

Guess 14

Actual Number 9

Bubble Gum, Bubble Gum

Making a set

This traditional rhyme transforms into a fun math activity. Place small colorful blocks (or linking cubes) in a bowl so they represent bubble gum. Lead students in chanting, "Bubble gum, bubble gum in a dish—how many pieces do you wish?" Prompt a child to roll a large foam die and count the dots. Have her announce the number and then remove that many pieces of bubble gum from the dish. Continue until all the bubble gum has been removed from the dish.

Marilyn Horsley
Valley View United Methodist Preschool
Overland Park, KS

Treasure Sets

Sorting, making equal sets

Youngsters search for unique buried treasure with this activity! Gather a set of four each of several common manipulatives, such as linking cubes, teddy bear counters, plastic bugs, seashells, and plastic links. Bury the manipulatives in your sand table. Youngsters work together to dig out the manipulatives and sort them by type. Then they make sure that there are four in each set. If not, they keep digging until each set is complete!

Suzanne Moore
Tucson, AZ

Which Is Heavier?

Exploring weight

Get a balance scale and several different sets of manipulatives. Gather several youngsters and have a child choose two different types of manipulatives. Ask, "Which one do you think will be heavier?" Have students make predictions. Then encourage students to help you count out equal sets of the manipulatives and place them on opposite sides of the scale. Encourage youngsters to compare their predictions to the result. Then repeat the process with different manipulatives.

Suzanne Moore

Super Snake!

Nonstandard measurement

Make a supersize boa constrictor cutout. (Or, if you or a parent sews, consider making a stuffed boa constrictor!) Place the boa constrictor on the floor and provide manipulatives, such as craft sticks. Throughout center time, encourage little ones to line up sticks next to the snake and then count the number of sticks. Switch out the manipulatives each day for added interest. Consider using linking cubes, plastic links, pipe cleaners, or wooden blocks!

Linda Barton; Busy Bees Child Care Center, LLC; Meriden, NH

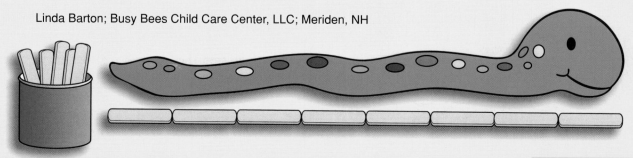

There's Math in the Forecast!

Build a foundation for addition and subtraction success with these weather-themed activities that are just perfect for preschoolers!

ideas contributed by Tricia Kylene Brown
Bowling Green, KY

Crazy Weather!
Counting

This weather forecast is packed full of every type of weather you can imagine! Cut out a copy of the weather cards on pages 230 and 231 and then attach them to your board. To begin, have youngsters count the images of weather on each card. Then lead students in the chant as you point to each card. If desired, have little ones make up a motion for each type of weather, such as holding their arms in a circle for the sun or clapping for the thunder. Then point to each card and guide youngsters in making the motions the appropriate number of times as they count aloud.

One big sun,
Two dark clouds,
Three claps of thunder:
Loud, loud, loud!
Four gusts of wind,
Five little flakes,
Six bolts of lightning
For goodness' sake!
Seven tiny twisters—
Imagine that!
Eight drops of rain:
Splat, splat, splat, splat,
Splat, splat, splat, splat!

Cloud Blowing
Separating sets

This activity also develops oral-motor skills! Gather a small group of youngsters. Then place between one and ten cotton balls (clouds) on a piece of blue construction paper (sky). Have little ones count the number of clouds. Then give each child a straw. Have her blow through her straw with her classmates to try and move the clouds out of the sky. After several seconds, signal for youngsters to stop. Then encourage youngsters to count how many clouds remain in the sky.

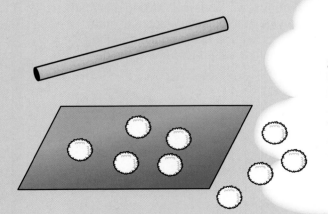

Snowflakes, Snowflakes!
Combining sets

Gather a supply of craft foam snowflakes. (For an alternative, punch hexagon cutouts from white craft foam so they resemble snowflakes.) Place the snowflakes in a container. Gather youngsters in a circle. Then give two children different sets of snowflakes, counting each snowflake aloud as you place it in her hands. Next, guide students in reciting the chant shown. Then have the two youngsters release their snowflakes in the middle of the circle and then join their classmates. Lead students in counting the snowflakes altogether. Pick up the snowflakes and play the game again!

Snowflakes, snowflakes—
Chilly, chilly weather!
How many flakes
Do you have altogether?

Tornado Take Away
Separating sets

Explain that tornadoes have been known to pick up things and then set them down again. Place between six and ten objects on the floor. Guide students in counting the objects. Then hold up a number card between one and five. Have students twirl around like a tornado that many times as you remove the same number of objects. Prompt little ones to sit. Then guide them in counting aloud the remaining objects.

Shake It!
Combining sets

Glue gray cloud cutouts to two tissue boxes. Place between one and five blue pom-poms (raindrops) in each box. Place a number line on a table. Ask a student to make it rain by turning the box upside-down and shaking it until all the raindrops fall out. Help him place the drops on the number line as he counts them aloud. Prompt a different child to repeat the process with the second box, adding the drops to the number line. Then help the students count all the raindrops on the number line. Encourage students to notice that the final number counted is the same as the numeral next to the final pom-pom.

| 1 | 2 | 3 | 4 | 5 | 6 | 7 | 8 | 9 | 10 |

1

TEC41071

2

TEC41071

3

TEC41071

4

TEC41071

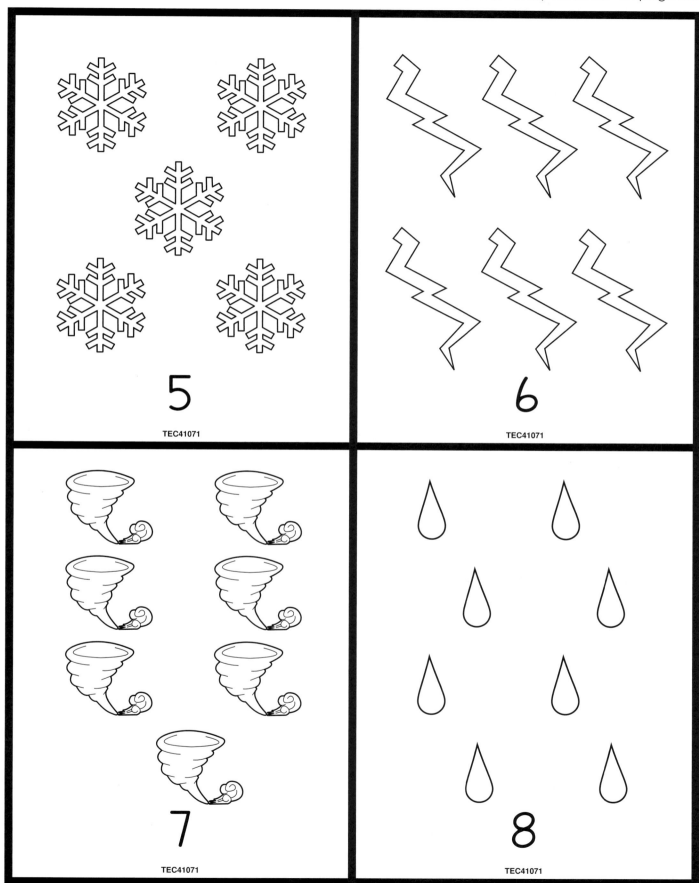

5

TEC41071

6

TEC41071

7

TEC41071

8

TEC41071

Sorting and Patterning Experiences

Give these math skills a workout with activities perfect
for anytime throughout the year.

Happy, Sad, Happy, Sad

Sorting, extending, and reading a pattern

Youngsters will have a ball sorting, patterning, and imitating these emotion
cards! Cut out several copies of the cards on page 234 and place the cards faceup
on the floor. Gather youngsters around the cards. Show youngsters one of the
happy cards and prompt them to imitate the emotion. Then show a sad card and
have little ones imitate that emotion. Guide youngsters to sort the cards into two
piles. Once the cards are sorted, begin a simple *AB* pattern on the floor. Encourage
little ones to extend the pattern. Then prompt them to read the pattern by
imitating the emotions. No doubt little ones will end up giggling!

Happy   Sad   Happy   Sad   Happy

Noodle This

Sorting and patterning by height

Pool noodle pieces make great manipulatives! Gather pool noodles and
cut them into pieces so there is a tall set and a short set. Place the pieces
at a center. Little ones visit the center and sort the pieces into two groups
by height. Then they experiment with arranging the pieces on the floor to
make patterns. Tall, short, tall, short, tall, short!

Lindsey Bachman
YWCA Early Learning Center
Duluth, MN

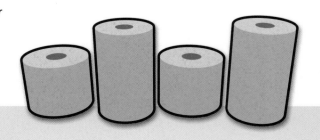

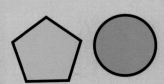

Old MacDonald's Farm

Participating in a song, sorting, reading a pattern

Old MacDonald certainly has a lot of critters on his farm! Color and cut out several copies of the cards on page 235. Give the cow and sheep cards to different children. Then lead students in singing the song shown, prompting children with cow cards to sit together in a group. Next, sing a second verse of the song, using sheep as the featured animal. Gather youngsters with the sheep cards in a separate group. Reinforce that the cows are in one group and the sheep are in another group. Finally, arrange the cows and sheep to begin a pattern. Have little ones help you extend the pattern. Then prompt little ones to help you read the pattern aloud, saying, "Moo, baa, moo, baa, moo, baa..." Repeat the activity with the chicken and pig cards.

"Old MacDonald Had a Farm"

Old MacDonald had a farm. *E, I, E, I, O!*
And on his farm, he had a [cow]. *E, I, E, I, O!*
With a [moo], [moo] here
And a [moo], [moo] there!
Here a [moo]; there a [moo];
Everywhere a [moo], [moo]!
Old MacDonald had a farm. *E, I, E, I, O!*

Got Stuff?

Sorting, patterning

Look no further for common manipulatives that are just perfect for sorting and patterning activities. Use these items to guide youngsters in whole-group sorting and patterning or for individual work at a center!

- Books (Sort and pattern by hardcover and paperback.)
- Clean, recyclable containers (Sort and pattern by cardboard and plastic.)
- Disposable plates (Sort and pattern by color or size.)
- Crayons (Sort and pattern by color.)
- Student pictures (Sort and pattern by sex.)
- Plastic utensils (Sort and pattern by type.)

Marie E. Cecchini
West Dundee, IL

Happy

TEC41072

Sad

TEC41072

Happy

TEC41072

Sad

TEC41072

TEC41072

TEC41072

TEC41072

TEC41072

A Whale of a Math Feature!

These math ideas will be a big hit with your little ones!

How Big?
Comparing size

Little ones think about the size of a whale with this no-prep idea! To begin, explain that whales are the largest animals on earth. A blue whale can grow to be as long as three school buses and its tongue on its own can weigh as much as an elephant! Name one of the objects below. If students think the object is bigger than a blue whale, have them stretch up on their tiptoes. If they think it is smaller than a blue whale, have them crouch down near the floor. Continue with the remaining objects.

Comparison objects: a pencil, a mountain, a car, a train, a school, a drinking straw, a lion, a city, a bed, a shoe, the United States, a ball

Roxanne LaBell Dearman
NC Intervention for the Deaf and Hard of Hearing
Charlotte, NC

Whale and Spout
Matching sets to numbers

Make several copies of the whale and spout patterns on page 238. Then label each whale with a set of dots and each spout with a corresponding number. Place the whales and spouts at a center. A visiting child chooses a whale and counts the dots. Then he finds the matching spout and places it above the whale. He continues with each remaining spout.

Sue Reppert, Widening World Preschool, Mentor, OH
Pat Wojciechowski, St. Albans Christian Learning Center, Sinking Spring, PA

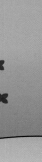

Five Big Whales!
Developing subtraction skills

Cut out five copies of the whale pattern on page 238 and attach them to a wall with tape. Have students count the whales. Then recite the first verse, removing a whale when appropriate and having students insert the correct number in the final line. Repeat the verse and remove a whale three more times. Then recite the final verse shown and remove the last whale.

[Five] big whales swimming to and fro—
Sometimes fast,
Sometimes slow.
One big whale said, "I'm off to get air!"
And that left [four whales] swimming there.

Final verse:
One big whale swimming to and fro—
Sometimes fast,
Sometimes slow.
That big whale said, "I'm off to get air!"
Now no more whales are swimming there.

adapted from an idea by Ruth Renedo, Adobe Christian Preschool, Petaluma, CA

Making Waves
Developing addition skills, using a number line

Cut blue scalloped bulletin board trim to make a length with 12 scallops. Number the trim as shown. Reduce the whale pattern on page 238 and then make a copy and cut it out. Get a die. Gather two youngsters. Have a child roll the die and count the dots. Then have him move the whale that many waves. Next, have his partner repeat the process, continuing the whale's journey. Have the youngsters notice what number the whale is on. Then remove the whale and play another round.

Cindy Hoying, Centerville, OH

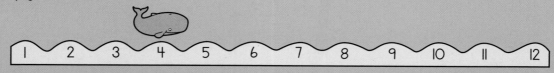

Tasty Fish
Identifying numbers

For each child, fold a blue paper plate in half so it resembles a whale's mouth. Give each child a whale mouth and a cup of fish crackers. Explain that some whales eat fish. Hold up a number card and have students identify the number. Then have them count and place the appropriate number of crackers in the whale's mouth. Continue for several rounds. Then have students nibble on their crackers.

Roxanne LaBell Dearman
NC Intervention for the Deaf and Hard of Hearing
Charlotte, NC

Whale and Spout Patterns

Use with "Whale and Spout" on page 236 and "Five Big Whales!" and "Making Waves" on page 237.

TEC41073

TEC41073

TEACHER RESOURCE UNITS

Happy Birthday, Alphabet!

Teach little ones letter names and sounds throughout the year with this engaging birthday theme! What a fun way to link something familiar with new learning!

ideas contributed by Catherine Mitchell, Littlest Angels Preschool, Brunswick, OH

Introduce the letter: Display a decorated cake cutout. Then post the focus letter on the cake. Have students sing happy birthday to the letter with a traditional birthday song, mentioning the name of the letter in the first singing and then the letter sound as they sing the song again. ***Reinforcing the letter name and sound***

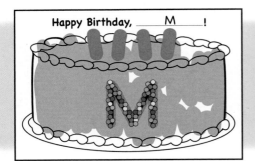

Happy Birthday, _____ M _____ !

A mini cake: Have each child color a copy of page 241 labeled with the focus letter. Encourage her to trace the letter with her finger and say its name. Then have her squeeze glue over the letter and sprinkle glitter, confetti, hole-punch dots, or other fun items on the glue. ***Letter formation***

Faux frosting: Squeeze fingerpaint (frosting) on a sheet of paper. Have a child sprinkle confetti on the paint and spread it over the paper as desired. Then encourage her to use her finger to write the focus letter in the paint. ***Letter formation***

Gift giving: Wrap a box with colorful birthday-themed paper and attach a colorful bow. Then help youngsters determine what presents the letter would like for its birthday, emphasizing that the presents should begin with the letter sound. ***Phonological awareness: beginning sounds***

Party hats: Cut small triangles from wrapping paper. Write letters on a sheet of chart paper, including several that match the focus letter. Encourage a child to point to a focus letter. Swipe a glue stick above the letter. Then have him press a triangle in the glue so it appears as if the letter is wearing a party hat! Continue in the same way. ***Letter identification***

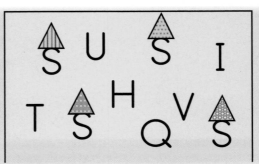

Birthday treats: Get a treat that begins with the focus letter. Then, with great fanfare, announce that the letter has brought in a birthday treat! Help students try to guess what the item might be. Then serve the treat, highlighting the beginning sound. The letter *S* brought in *strawberries*! ***Letter-sound association***

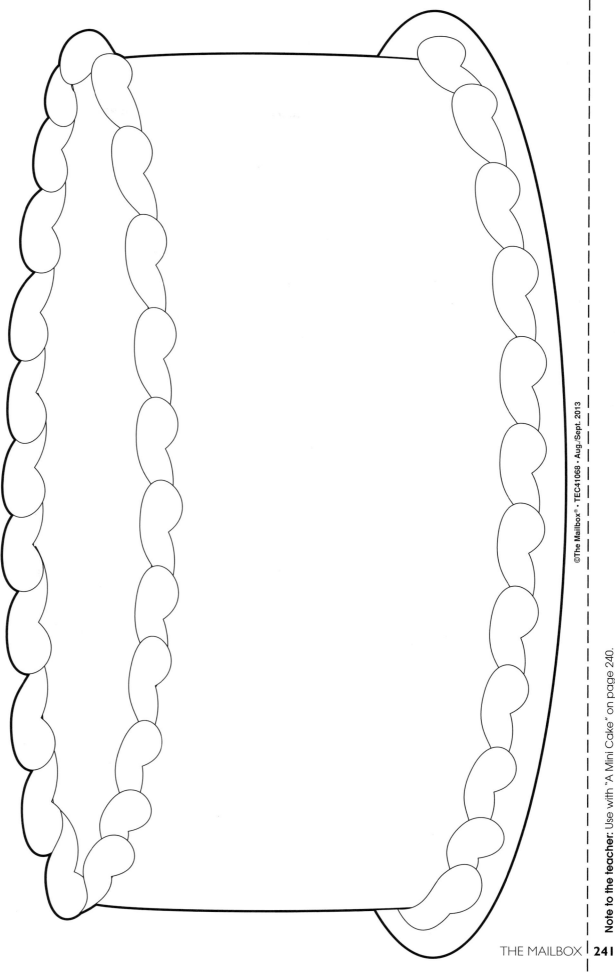

Happy Birthday, _____ !

©The Mailbox® · TEC41068 · Aug./Sept. 2013

Note to the teacher: Use with "A Mini Cake" on page 240.

4 Songs to Sing and Sign!

Here's a selection of simple songs with sign language actions!

1 Letters and Sounds

Here's a ditty that reinforces letter signs and letter sounds! Lead students in singing the song and making the hand sign for the letter *A* each time they say the letter and when they make the letter sound. Repeat the song several times with other letters.

(sung to the tune of "London Bridge")

Letter [*A*], what do you say,
Do you say, do you say?
Letter [*A*], what do you say?
[/a/, /a/, /a/, /a/]!

Laura Corgan
Christ Lutheran Children's Center
Charlotte, NC

A

THUMP
THUMP

pumpkin

here

2 Where's My Pumpkin?

Spotlight fall with this simple song and these signs!

(sung to the tune of "Where Is Thumbkin?")

Where's my pumpkin?
Where's my pumpkin?

Here it is!
Here it is!

What a perfect pumpkin.
What a perfect pumpkin.

Happy fall.
Happy fall.

Cindy Kelley
St. Bernard School
Wabash, IN

fall

eye

ear

nose

tongue

hands

3 Our Senses!

Lead youngsters in singing the song, inserting the eye sign and the word *see* when appropriate. Repeat the song four more times with the options given.

(sung to the tune of "The Farmer in the Dell")

We use our [eye sign] to [see].
We use our [eye sign] to [see].
Heigh-ho the derry-o!
We use our [eye sign] to [see].

Continue with the following:
ear sign/*hear*
nose sign/*smell*
tongue sign/*taste*
hands sign/*touch*

Terrie Solesbee
Trinity Presbyterian Rainbow Club
Flower Mound, TX

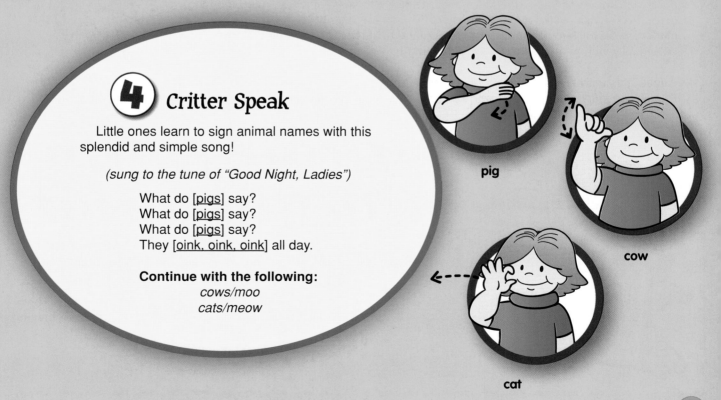

4 Critter Speak

Little ones learn to sign animal names with this splendid and simple song!

(sung to the tune of "Good Night, Ladies")

What do [pigs] say?
What do [pigs] say?
What do [pigs] say?
They [oink, oink, oink] all day.

Continue with the following:
cows/*moo*
cats/*meow*

pig

cow

cat

Time to Talk!

Encourage speaking skills with this selection of easy-to-implement ideas!

Ideas contributed by Roxanne LaBell Dearman
NC Early Intervention Program for Students Who Are Deaf or Hard of Hearing
Charlotte, NC

Good Morning!

Help little ones take conversational cues and learn friendly phrases with this simple activity! Attach a sun cutout to a craft stick. Ask little ones if anyone has ever said "good morning" to them. Encourage youngsters to share their experiences. Explain that when someone says "good morning," it's polite to smile and say "good morning" in return. Practice with several youngsters. Then show little ones the sun puppet. Tell students you will show them the sun puppet the next morning to remind them to reply individually when you tell them "good morning"!

Repeat this activity with a smiley face puppet and the question "How are you?" Encourage students to answer with sentences such as "I am fine. How are you?"

Tell a Story

Place wordless picture books in your reading center along with a supply of dolls and stuffed toys. Tell youngsters that the toys would love to hear a story. Then encourage little ones to visit the center and take a toy and a book. The child "reads" the story to the toy. Then she chooses a new toy and book!

What's in the Box?

Gather several unique pictures and random items, such as tongs, a key, a wrench, a photo of a volcano, and a photo of a camel. Place the items in a box. Each day, show youngsters an item or picture. Pass it around, prompting each child to say something she knows or would like to know about the item.

Phone a Friend

Little ones don't need real phones to encourage phone conversational rules! Gather a variety of props that can be used as imaginary phones, such as two plastic bananas, two plastic cups, two pieces of PVC pipe, or two wooden blocks. (Flat-sided wooden blocks work particularly well as pretend smartphones!) Store the items in a tub labeled "Fun Phones." Encourage students to take a pair of phones and have a conversation. Remind them to take turns, ask questions, and say "hello" and "goodbye."

What Are They Saying?

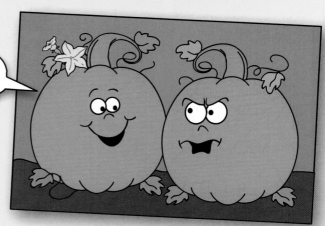

This little visual is sure to get youngsters talking! Color a copy of page 246 and display it in your circle-time area. Ask a child what he thinks the pumpkins are saying. Then encourage other youngsters to describe different conversations the two pumpkins could have.

©The Mailbox® • TEC41069 • Oct./Nov. 2013

Note to the teacher: Use with "What Are They Saying?" on page 245.

Teacher Bag of Tricks

"Quick," you say. "I need a zippy idea to focus my youngsters' attention!" Here you go! Put these ideas in your bag of tricks to pull out when needed.

concept contributed by Sylvia Sonnier, Academy of the Sacred Heart, Grand Coteau, LA

★ Encourage little ones to lie down. Dim the classroom lights and then lead them in singing a quiet round of **"Twinkle, Twinkle, Little Star."** Then, whispering, explain to youngsters what activity is coming next.

★ Play a quick game of **thumbs-up and thumbs-down**. Say statements such as "I like pizza." Each youngster who likes pizza gives a thumbs-up. Each child who doesn't gives a thumbs-down. This can also be played with color cards. Hold up a color card and name a color. If you've identified the color on the card correctly, each youngster gives a thumbs-up. If not, she gives a thumbs-down. *LeeAnn Collins, Sunshine House Preschool, Lansing, MI*

★ Slowly recite **"Pease Porridge Hot"** while students alternate clapping their hands and patting their legs. When finished, help students name two other words that begin with /p/. Recite the rhyme again, substituting the two new words for *pease* and *porridge*. Purple pants hot!

★ Play a quick game of **"Elephant and Mouse."** Have students stand and march as an elephant would march. Then encourage them to march like mice. Repeat the activity, having youngsters tiptoe, stomp, jump, wiggle, and then sit like both elephants and mice.

★ Grab a handful of pom-poms. Say, **"How many?"** Have students guess how many pom-poms you're holding. Then count them one at a time, giving each counted pom-pom to a student to place back in the tub.

★ Chant several rounds of the **wiggle rhyme** below, substituting different body parts and having students wiggle their bodies when indicated. *Rexann Roussel, Narrow Acres Preschool, Paulina, LA*

Put your hands on your [head].
Put your hands on your [head].
Put your hands on your [head]
And wiggle, wiggle, wiggle!

Going From Here to There: 10 Transition Ideas

Need fun and skill-related ideas to transition to center time? To naptime? To hand washing? Look no further!

1 Gather a class supply of colorful items—like pom-poms, bear counters, or building blocks—and conceal them in a sack. Have each child take an item from the sack. Then call youngsters to line up according to the color of their items. As each child lines up, collect the item. *Nicole Ingegneri, Sydenstricker United Methodist Church Tot Preschool, Springfield, VA*

2 Post in your group area sticky notes labeled with uppercase or lowercase letters that your class is working on. Invite each child (letter detective) to find a note and identify the letter as uppercase or lowercase. Then send her on her way! *Nicole Furfaro, St. Paul Catholic School, Guelph, Ontario, Canada*

3 Attach a handle to a cardboard canister and then decorate it with fun stickers and craft materials. Place cards programmed with favorite classroom song titles inside the canister. Then use this crafty transition tote as a musical time filler, whether in the classroom or on the go! *Jennifer Gemar, Tripp-Delmont Elementary, Tripp, SD*

Twinkle, Twinkle, Little Star

4 Have children count off in numerical order or say the alphabet in sequential order as they line up or move on to another activity. For a cultural twist, have youngsters say the numbers or the alphabet in a different language! *Kime Lima, Lab Children's Center, Livermore, CA*

5 Hand out musical instruments as youngsters line up. Then, using a craft stick baton, direct students to play loudly or softly as the group transitions to its destination! *Ashley Foster, Tendercare Learning Center, Clairton, PA*

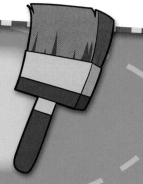

6 Keep a class supply of inexpensive paintbrushes in a bucket. Then have little ones put on imaginary paint smocks, take a brush, and "paint" whatever they like in the room. When it's time to move on, children return the brushes to the bucket, and they're ready to go! *Mrs. Cosgrove, South Windsor Child Development Center, South Windsor, CT*

7 Write different numbers on individual sheets from a decorative (or seasonal) notepad. Place the sheets facedown on the floor and have each child take one. Then call out one of the numbers. Have the child with that number give you his note and transition on. Continue with each number. *Becky Winter, South Georgia Elementary, Amarillo, TX*

8 Place assorted die-cuts—such as a dinosaur, a dog, a horse, and a fish—in a bag. When it's time to line up, take a die-cut from the bag and announce student names and a shape-related direction for them to perform as they line up. For example, say, "Stomp like a dinosaur," "Pant like a dog," "Gallop like a horse," or "Swim like a fish!" *Susan Luengen, Makalapa Elementary School, Honolulu, HI*

9 For this transition activity, grab some pom-poms from a bag and toss them onto the floor. Lead youngsters in counting the pom-poms and then send that many children on their way! *Linda Heavrin, Benton, IL*

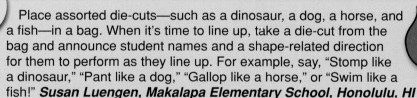

10 Use this transitional departure rhyme to highlight classroom responsibility. Recite the rhyme, inserting a task like "the tables are clean." Then help youngsters scan the room to see if the task is done. If it is, give little ones a round of applause. If not, ask a volunteer to complete the task. *Kim Love, Territorial Elementary, Chino Valley, AZ*

School is done; [cleaning task].
The room must look just so.
Let's give a check to be sure—
It's almost time to go!

Tap BOOM Ding!

Exploring Music

Clap, Pat, Stomp, and Walk

Youngsters feel the beat of a piece of music in different ways with this easy idea! Have students sit in a circle. Then play a musical recording and encourage little ones to clap to the beat. Next, have students tap their legs to the beat. Encourage youngsters to stand. Then have them stomp to the beat. Finally, have students walk in a circle to the beat.

Suzanne Moore
Tucson, AZ

A Musical Adventure!

Choose a specific material, such as aluminum foil, tissue paper, corrugated cardboard, or Bubble Wrap cushioning material. Then encourage students to discover what kind of percussive noises can be made with the material. For example, students can roll a square of aluminum foil and use it like a kazoo, cover an open container and tap it like a drum, or cover wooden blocks and listen to the noise they make when knocked together. What a fun exploration!

Marcell Gibison
Ephrata Church of the Brethren Children's Center
Ephrata, PA

Fast and Slow

To help youngsters focus on the tempo of music, give each child a crepe paper streamer. (For an extra-sturdy version, attach the streamer to a paint stirring stick and have little ones use the stick as a handle.) Play upbeat music and encourage little ones to move the streamer through the air to reflect the fast rhythm of the song. Next, play a slow song and prompt students to move the streamer through the air with slow and gentle movements.

Suzanne Moore, Tucson, AZ
Peggy Riffle, Lansing Christian Preschool, Lansing, MI

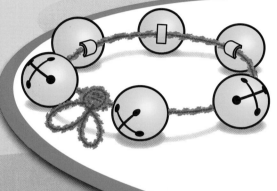

Jingle Stompers

For extra fun adding movement to music, have little ones wear jingle stompers! To make a jingle stomper, thread jingle bells onto a pipe cleaner. Then lightly wrap the pipe cleaner around a child's ankle and twist the ends to secure it. Play a selection of upbeat music and encourage little ones to dance. They'll love hearing the jingling accompaniment!

Suzanne Moore

Keep the Beat

Have little ones sit in a circle. Then give one child a tambourine. Play music with a strong, consistent beat and encourage the child to tap the tambourine to the beat. Then have him pass the tambourine to the next child, who repeats the process. When youngsters are comfortable with this activity, introduce another instrument to the circle, such as shakers.

Sarah Sant
First Baptist Church Preschool
Sulphur Springs, TX

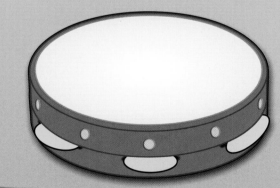

So Much Variety!

Gather samples of different types of music, such as classical, folk, Celtic, African, and opera. Then play one type each day for several days. At the end of the time period, play a quick reminder of each music type. Then help youngsters measure their favorite type using sticky notes on a floor graph. (For extra fun, have students use music note die-cuts instead of sticky notes!)

Mary Stieveling, Bay Shore, NY

CHEZ PREK CAFÉ:
Teaching Table Manners

Transform a special snacktime into a fancy restaurant experience with these ideas! What a fun way to teach social skills!

ideas contributed by Terri Wright
Little Darlings Child Care Center of Philadelphia
Philadelphia, PA

Before

- Get two snack options, such as cheese slices and crackers, in addition to plates and napkins.
- List the snack menu on a chalkboard that says "Chez PreK Café."
- Place a tablecloth on each table.
- Have little ones decorate empty water bottles (vases) and make paper flowers. Then place a flower in each vase and put them on the tables.
- Review table manners with youngsters using the cards on page 253.
- Have little ones wash their hands.

During

- Dim the lights and play classical music.
- Put a towel over your arm and serve snacks as if youngsters were at a fancy restaurant. Ask little ones if they want only one of the snack items or both, prompting them to say, "Please." (Using the titles "Miss" and "Mr." when talking to the students will certainly elicit some giggles!)
- Encourage each child to say, "Thank you," when she receives her snack.
- Remind students to place their napkins in their laps.

After

- Encourage students to pretend they are leaving the restaurant. Have them suggest some kind words they could say to a waiter or waitress when they leave.
- Discuss what grown-ups do when it is time to leave the restaurant (pay the bill, leave a tip, etc.). Ask, "What is a tip, and why do we leave one?"

7 SUPER Gross-Motor Time Fillers!

1

Preschool Puppies Tell your little ones to pretend to be puppies. Then instruct them to do a variety of puppy tricks, like rolling over, begging, sitting, jumping, running, and barking. Finally, encourage them to take a much-needed puppy nap! *Roxanne LaBell Dearman, NC Intervention for the Deaf and Hard of Hearing, Charlotte, NC*

2

Stretch to the Clouds Have little ones reach up and encourage them to "grab" a big, fluffy cloud. Once they grab a cloud, have them "feel" how soft and puffy it is and then "drag" it to the floor. Have them repeat the process, dragging a bunch of clouds to the floor. Finally, have them reach down, grab all of the clouds, and then "throw" them back up into the sky! *Mindi Morton, Mindi's Oak Tree Preschool, North San Juan, CA*

3

Left and Right Make a sign labeled "left" and a sign labeled "right." Then display them appropriately in your classroom for youngsters to use as a reference. Have little ones spread out. Then say, "Left!" and encourage them to jump to the left. Say, "Right!" and prompt them to jump to the right. Continue in the same way in a random fashion. When students get the hang of this, add "Up!" and have them stand on their tiptoes, and "Down!" encouraging them to crouch near the floor. *Amy Crawford, Virginia Beach, VA*

4

Stop! Play a musical recording and have students move in a circle. As they move, hold up shape cutouts, encouraging them to shout out the name of the shape. If you hold up an octagon, students stop and freeze. What a fun way to reinforce the shape of a stop sign!
Susan Perry, Avon Nursery School, Avon, MA

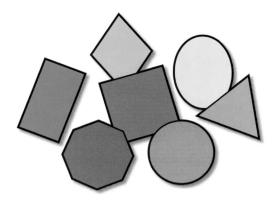

5

Snappy Alligator Have students sit in a circle. Then choose a child (alligator) to sit in the middle of the circle and pretend to take a nap. Have a volunteer walk across the circle near the alligator as youngsters recite the rhyme shown. The child moves quickly to reach the other side before the alligator "wakes up" and snaps (moves his arms like snapping jaws). That child becomes the next alligator. Change the gross-motor movement for each round. *Tysha Rivich, Innovations in Learning, Hobart, IN*

> Alligator, alligator, taking a nap,
> I'll [walk] by you before you snap!

Continue with the following: *march, tiptoe, gallop, crawl, jog*

6

Can't Stand Up! This quick time filler is sure to produce a lot of giggles! Have each youngster hold his own wrists with the opposite hands. Then encourage him to try to stand up. It isn't easy! Next, have him sit down the same way. Ask youngsters whether it's easier to stand up or sit down.
Keely Saunders, Bonney Lake Early Childhood Education Assistance Program, Bonney Lake, WA

7

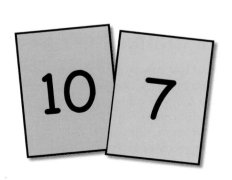

Do the Flamingo Get a stack of number cards. Then have a child choose a card. Challenge youngsters to stand on one foot like a flamingo while they count aloud to that number. If a child loses his balance, he sits on his flamingo nest until the next round. *Roxanne LaBell Dearman, NC Intervention for the Deaf and Hard of Hearing, Charlotte, NC*

Staying Safe: Stranger Danger

Help little ones identify safe and unsafe strangers with these important activities!

Who Can I Trust?

Telling the difference between a helpful stranger and a dangerous stranger can be confusing! Give students some guidelines with this activity. Name a type of stranger (see the lists below). Prompt children to say the rhyme shown if they think there is stranger danger. If not, have students say, "Safe!"

> That's a grown-up I don't know.
> It's not safe—I will not go!

Safe strangers: the school nurse, your teacher, a police officer, a firefighter, a sales clerk in a store, a doctor in a doctor's office

Unsafe strangers: a grown-up asking you to help find a lost animal, a grown-up offering you a ride, a grown-up offering you candy

It's a Wolf!

Make a copy of the patterns on page 257 and transform them into stick puppets. Read aloud a version of *Little Red Riding Hood*, prompting students to identify the stranger in the story *(the wolf)*. After the story, review what Red does when she meets the wolf and what she should have done differently. Next, give a child the Red Riding Hood puppet. Hold the wolf puppet and have the wolf ask, "Little Red, why don't you come with me into the woods?" Encourage the child to have Little Red say, "No! I will not go!" Have the child give the puppet to a classmate. Then continue with a different request, such as "Little Red, I have some tasty candy for you. Please come with me!" Play several rounds. If desired, have youngsters make their own puppets to take home.

Jan Trautman
Pleasant Union Elementary
Raleigh, NC

Strangers

Not So Strange!

Help little ones understand that dangerous strangers might not look so strange. Write "Strangers" on a sheet of chart paper. Then have students cut out pictures of grown-ups from magazines and attach them to the paper. Have youngsters notice how the strangers look very nice, friendly, and attractive. Ask, "If a stranger is pretty, does that mean the stranger is safe?" Have students share their thoughts, guiding them to understand that dangerous strangers don't necessarily look like bad people.

TEC41073

TEC41073

Make a copy of pages 258–260 for each child. Help each child follow the directions for each page. Then staple the pages together.

Booklet pages 1 and 2: Color the pages. Make fingerprint leaves on the trees and ground. Draw a face and hair on the child.

2

Long sleeves.

1

Colorful leaves.

Booklet pages 3 and 4: Color the pages. Glue cotton-batting whipped cream to the pie. Make a brown fingerprint football in the air. Use a fine-tip marker to draw lacing details on the football.

4

Footballs fly!

3

Pumpkin pie.

6

And turkey too!

5

A friendly "Boo!"

BOO!

Make a copy of pages 261–263 for each child. Help each child follow the directions for each page. Then cut out the pages and staple them together.
Cover and booklet page 1: Color the pages, including the sky on page 1.
Make fingerprints (snowflakes) with white paint on the first page.

My Winter Senses

by _____

©The Mailbox® • TEC41070 • Dec./Jan. 2013–14

I see snowflakes.

1

I hear a crackling fire.

2

I taste hot cocoa.

3

Booklet pages 4 and 5: Color the pages. Squeeze glue on the gingerbread people and then sprinkle cinnamon on the glue. Glue two felt mitten cutouts to the page.

I smell gingerbread.

4

I feel mittens.

5

Make a copy of pages 264–266 for each child. Help her follow the directions for each page. Then help her cut out the pages and staple them together.

Cover and booklet page 1: Color the cover and booklet page. Then use glitter glue to trace the flight paths of the bees.

It Is Spring!

by _____

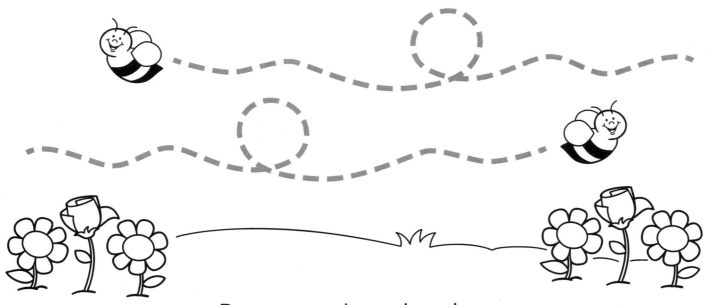

Bees are buzzing by.
It is spring!

1

Booklet pages 2 and 3: Color the pages. Stretch cotton balls and glue them to the clouds on booklet page 2. Make fingerprint raindrops on booklet page 3.

Kites fly in the sky.
It is spring!

2

Rain is falling down.
It is spring!

3

Booklet pages 4 and 5: Color the pages. Make fingerprint tulips on booklet page 4. Mix glitter with glue and brush it on the sun on booklet page 5.

Flowers can be found.
It is spring!

4

The sun warms everything!
It is spring!

5

THEMATIC UNITS

A Really BIG Preschool Welcome!

Welcome little ones to preschool with these dinosaur-themed activities, and you'll hear roars of approval!

Where to Sit?

Group-time seating

Help little ones take a seat during group time with this simple idea! Make a class supply of colorful dinosaur footprints from craft foam. If desired, label each footprint with a different child's name. Then scatter the footprints in your group-time area. Encourage each child to find a footprint (or his personalized footprint) and then sit on it.

adapted from an idea by Pat Wojciechowski
St. Albans Christian Learning Center
Sinking Spring, PA

Dino Dig

Attendance

Write a dinosaur version of each child's name on different bone cutouts. Then highlight each name so it stands out. Attach a piece of brown bulletin board paper to a wall (dinosaur dig site). Attach the hook side of Velcro fasteners to the paper. Then attach the loop side of Velcro fasteners to the bones. On the first day of school, introduce youngsters to their dinosaur names. Then scatter the bones on a table before each school day. When a child arrives, he finds his dinosaur name and attaches it to the dinosaur dig site.

Evelyn Harmon
Franklin Children's School
Franklin, MA

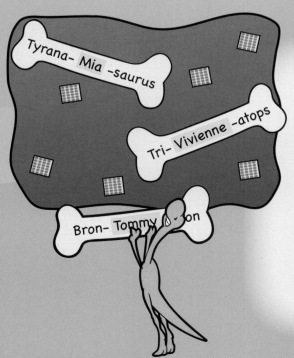

Stomp and Roar!

Get-acquainted activity

Help little ones identify their own names as well as those of their classmates with this excellent action chant! Write each child's name on a different dinosaur cutout (see page 271). Then have youngsters stand in a circle. Display a dinosaur as you lead them in reciting the chant, stomping when they say "stomp" and roaring the word *roar.* Then help youngsters identify the name on the dinosaur and locate that classmate. Continue with the remaining dinosaurs.

Give a stomp!
Give a roar!
Whose name's on this dinosaur?

Lots of Dino Fun!

Centers

Look no further for engaging center options for this popular theme!

- **Fine motor:** Explain that archaeologists have to carefully dig through the dirt to find dinosaur bones. Then give each child a chocolate chip cookie. Have her pretend to be an archaeologist as she uses a toothpick to carefully dig out the chocolate chips!
- **Discovery:** Place a brown blanket on a tabletop. Then add houseplants, plastic dinosaur toys, large rocks, and blue cellophane pieces (lakes and ponds). Youngsters explore this dinosaur landscape.
- **Play dough:** Provide plastic dinosaur toys and encourage students to press the dinosaurs into the play dough to make footprints.
- **Art:** Press plastic dinosaur toys in shallow pans of paint and then on paper. Continue with other dinosaur toys and colors of paint.

Evelyn Harmon, Franklin Children's School, Franklin, MA

Got Books?

Here are some fabulous dinosaur storytime selections that are just perfect for your preschool class!

Dinosaurs, Dinosaurs by Byron Barton
Dinosaurumpus! by Tony Mitton
Ten Terrible Dinosaurs by Paul Stickland
Dinosaur Roar! by Paul and Henrietta Stickland

So Sorry!

Song

Introduce youngsters to the word *extinct*, explaining that *extinct* refers to a type of animal or plant that has died out, such as dinosaurs. Then lead youngsters in this giggle-inducing song! If desired, show students a photo of each type of dinosaur mentioned. (An Internet image search turns up a variety of options.)

(sung to the tune of "Clementine")

[*Stegosaurus, Stegosaurus*],
You're my favorite dinosaur.
I'm so sorry you're extinct now.
You're not living anymore.

Continue with the following: *Tyrannosaurus, Apatosaurus, Ankylosaurus, Comptosaurus*

Sandra Williams
L. Frances Smith Elementary
Columbus, IN

Story Walk

Literacy project

Spotlight sequencing skills with this simple project! Encourage each child to color the cards on a copy of page 272 as desired. Help her cut out the cards and arrange them in order on a 4" x 18" strip of paper. Then have her glue the cards in place. Next, have her take a plastic dinosaur and "walk" it over the cards from left to right as she tells the story.

Evelyn Harmon, Franklin Children's School
Franklin, MA

 Help little ones line up with this simple trick! Cut out a class supply of colorful dinosaur patterns on page 271. Attach them to a wall in a row. Each youngster stands next to a different dinosaur and then places a finger on her dinosaur. When the line is straight, have students place their hands at their sides and get ready to walk!

Dinosaur Patterns

Use with "Stomp and Roar!" on page 269, with the tip on page 270, and for cubby labels and nametags.

TEC41068

TEC41068

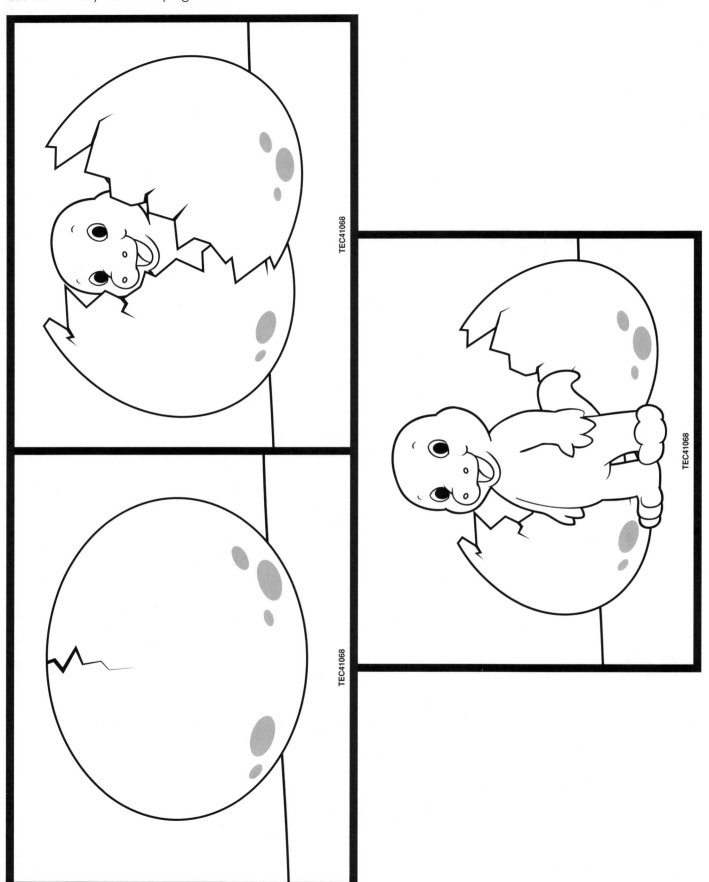

TEC41068

TEC41068

TEC41068

I Can Be a Friend!

Emphasize friendship skills with this selection of activities!

Sunny Words
Dictating information

Good friends use positive words. Help reinforce those words with this sunny idea! Attach a sunny cutout and a gray cloud cutout to a wall. Tell students that sunny words are words we can say that make others happy and cloudy words are words that make others feel sad. Help students come up with examples of these two types of words and write their suggestions on the cutouts. Encourage sunny words in daily interactions. If desired, spotlight youngsters that use sunny words by giving them sun-ray bracelets (strips of yellow construction paper fashioned into bracelets) or sun hand stamps.

Barb Dover, Giggly Wiggly Preschool, Issaquah, WA

I like you.
Good work!
You have pretty shoes.
Let's play blocks.

You're not my friend.
You look ugly.
I won't play with you.

Clap Your Hands!
Gross-motor skills

Lead students in singing this engaging song that emphasizes caring and sharing friendships. Repeat the song several times, substituting the clapping with the movements mentioned.

(sung to the tune of "If You're Happy and You Know It")

[Clap your hands] if you're a friend, [clap your hands]!   *Clap twice.*
[Clap your hands] if you're a friend, [clap your hands]!   *Clap twice.*
I'm a friend because I share; I'm a friend because I care.
[Clap your hands] if you're a friend, [clap your hands]!   *Clap twice.*

Continue with the following: *stomp your feet, pat your head, slap your legs, shake your hips*

Suzanne Moore, Tucson, AZ

Gossie and Gertie
Recognizing story events

Cut out a copy of the cards on page 275 and get the book *Gossie and Gertie* by Olivier Dunrea. Gossie and Gertie are best friends, and they do everything together. Gossie says, "Follow me!" and Gertie follows—until Gertie decides to do her own thing. To begin, explain that friends like to do things together. Ask, "What can you do with a friend?" Have students share their thoughts. Then read the story aloud. Next, place the cards facedown on the floor. Encourage a child to turn over a card. Read it aloud. Then have students identify whether this is something Gossie and Gertie do together. (Use the book's illustrations as a reference when needed.) Continue with each remaining card.

Of course you'll be looking for more feathered friendship fun! Have little ones compare Gossie and Gertie to Duck and Goose on page 151! How are the pairs of friends different?

Friendship Painting
Cooperation

Place two attached white paper towels in a container with high sides. Provide a variety of paintbrushes. Have two little friends stand next to the container and encourage each child to choose a brush. Then have them dip their brushes into tinted water and flick, drizzle, and drip the water onto the paper towels. Prompt youngsters to continue with different brushes. When the project is dry, separate the paper towels so each child can take home a portion of the project.

Janet Boyce, Cokato, MN

Friendly Behavior
Participating in a song

Promote friendly behavior with this catchy ditty!

(sung to the tune of "The Wheels on the Bus")

I can be a friend by [sharing toys],
[Sharing toys], [sharing toys].
I can be a friend by [sharing toys]
Every day!

Continue with the following: *giving help, being kind, giving hugs*

Suzanne Moore, Tucson, AZ

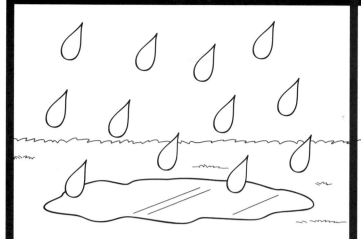

They splash in the rain.

TEC41068

They play in the daisies.

TEC41068

They watch at night.

TEC41068

They play in the haystacks.

TEC41068

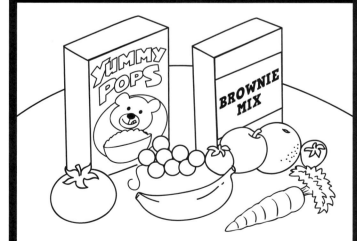

They go to the store.

TEC41068

They play with the pig.

TEC41068

Hooray for FALL!

It's time for beautiful leaves, plump pumpkins, and all things autumn!

Green No Longer!

Developing fine-motor skills, investigating seasonal characteristics

Help youngsters remember the most vibrant fall characteristic with this simple activity! Gather a small group of children and give each child a green leaf cutout. Ask students to explain what happens to leaves during the fall, encouraging them to explain that the leaves change colors. Then prompt them to name the colors of fall leaves. Next, have each child paint his green leaf orange, red, yellow, and brown. Fall is here!

Cori Marinan, Howe School, Green Bay, WI

Fall Is Not Easy

Responding to a story through art

Read aloud *Fall Is Not Easy* by Marty Kelley. In this simple rhyming story, a tree has difficulty getting its leaves to change to the appropriate colors. It has rainbow leaves, smiley face leaves, and polka-dot leaves. Then, when the tree finally gets it right, the leaves all fall off and winter arrives! After the read-aloud, have each child use watercolors to paint grass and a tree trunk on a sheet of paper. Then encourage her to make her own confused tree by adding colorful craft items to the project to make foliage. Display the resulting projects with the title "Fall Is Not Easy!"

Real or Fake?

Investigating living things

For this discovery center, place real and fake fall leaves in a container and then place the container at a table. Attach a real leaf and fake leaf to separate empty baskets and place them on either side of the container along with the labels shown. Provide a magnifying glass. Youngsters explore the leaves and sort them according to whether they are real or fake.

Melissa Fary
Kensington School of the Highlands
LaGrange, IL

Real Fake

Are the leaves real or fake?

Pumpkin Positions

Positional words

In advance, make a booklet for each child with five copies of the booklet page on page 279. Label the pages *in*, *next to*, *under*, *on*, and *between*. Gather two disposable cups and place one upside down and the other right-side up. Get a small group of youngsters and give a child an orange pom-pom (pumpkin). Ask him to place the pumpkin in a cup. Repeat the process, having different youngsters place the pumpkin next to, under, on, and between the cups. Next, give each child a booklet. Have her make a fingerprint pumpkin in the appropriate place on each page. Then have her draw a stem on each pumpkin.

Mary Ann Craven, Fallbrook United Methodist School, Fallbrook, CA

in

on

between

Not-So-Spooky Snack!

Following directions

To make this cute and simple trail mix snack, provide a bowl of pretzel sticks (broomsticks), mini chocolate chips (bat's eyes), and harvest moons (puffed corn cereal). Have each child place a scoop of each item into a resealable plastic bag. Then encourage him to munch on his Halloween treat!

Cindy Bryan, Creative Learning Center
Springfield, MO

Fall Shaker Fun
Investigating the five senses

These sensory bottles can be used for a discovery center or as an accompaniment to fall-themed songs. (For a particularly fun choice, see "Fa-la-la Fall!" on page 135.) Place loose feed corn, acorns, and pumpkin seeds in a small clean soda bottle. Secure the lid with heavy-duty tape or hot glue. Then encourage youngsters to manipulate the bottles to observe the contents.

Erin McGinness
Great New Beginnings Early Learning Center
Bear, DE

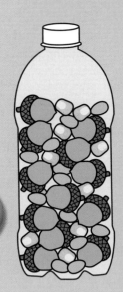

For extra fun, place letter tiles in the bottle to spell *fall.* Provide a sheet of paper with the word *fall* written on it. Then prompt a child to manipulate the bottle and cross out the letters as he sees them.

Thanksgiving Day Is Coming!
Exploring characteristics of a holiday
Spotlight Thanksgiving Day activities with this cute song!

(sung to the tune of "Skip to My Lou")

Thanksgiving is coming! What will we do?
Thanksgiving is coming! What will we do?
Thanksgiving is coming! What will we do?
Thanksgiving Day is coming!

Continue with the following:
Family's together—hip hip hooray! (Final line: Family's all together!)
Turkey's in the oven—yum, yum, yum! (Final line: Turkey's in the oven.)
Tummy's all full—no room for pie! (Final line: Tummy is all full.)
Time for a nap—shhhh, shhhh, shhhh! (Final line: Thank you for Thanksgiving!)

Rita Grube, Fairlawn Preschool, Columbus, IN

Fall Faces
Working cooperatively

Place a vinyl tablecloth on a table and then use a permanent marker to draw a large circle on the tablecloth. Provide a basket with fall leaves, pinecones, twigs, gourds, Indian corn, and mini pumpkins. Two youngsters visit the center and place items on the circle to make a fall-themed face. What fun! If desired, take a photo of each face, make a large printout, and then post it in the classroom.

Tricia Kylene Brown, Bowling Green, KY

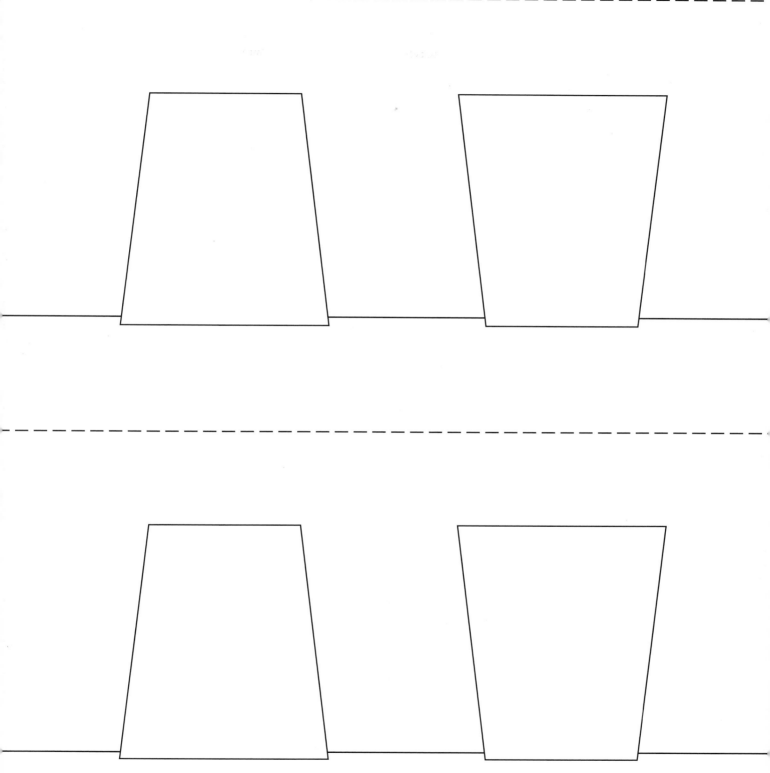

Warm, Fragrant, and Perfect for Winter—It's Gingerbread Time!

Listen and Do
Following directions

Gather a small group of youngsters and give each child a copy of page 282. Then read aloud the first direction below. Observe youngsters as they choose the correct crayon and follow the direction. Continue with each direction in the same way.

Heather Rawlings, Gateway Kids Preschool, Murrieta, CA

Directions:
1. Pick up a blue crayon. Color the door.
2. Pick up a red crayon. Color one candy red.
3. Pick up a purple crayon. Color two candies purple.
4. Pick up a green crayon. Color one candy green.
5. Pick up an orange crayon. Color one candy orange.
6. Pick up a brown crayon. Color the rest of the picture.

Life Cycle of a Gingerbread Man
Sequencing a story

The life of a gingerbread man is a short one indeed! Accordion-fold a 6" x 18" strip of paper for each child. Give him a copy of the cards on page 283 and an accordion-folded booklet. Have him color the cards and then cut them out. Then encourage him to arrange the cards in order. After you check the order, have him glue the cards in order in the booklet.

Sheryl Keseian, Avon Nursery School, Avon, MA

Marvelous Mix!
Exploring the senses of touch and smell

Ask parents to provide boxes of gingerbread mix. Then empty the boxes in your sensory table! Provide measuring cups, measuring spoons, sieves, and plastic bowls. Then encourage students to explore this scented table filler!

Darlene Taig
Willow Creek Cooperative Preschool
Westland, MI

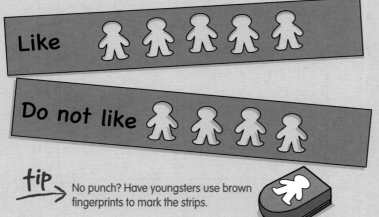

tip → No punch? Have youngsters use brown fingerprints to mark the strips.

Smelly!
Organizing data

Obtain a gingerbread man–shaped paper punch and a piece of ginger root or a container of ground ginger. Also label two strips of brown paper as shown. Gather a small group of youngsters and explain that one of the ingredients in gingerbread is a spice called ginger. Have each youngster smell the ginger, determine whether he likes the smell, and then use the punch on the appropriate strip. When each child has had an opportunity, have students discuss the results.

adapted from an idea by Ellen Maguire
Little Corner School House
Brookline, MA

Making Friends!
Responding to a story through art

In advance, place gingerbread men cookie cutters at a table along with shallow pans of brown paint and construction paper. To begin, read aloud *Gingerbread Friends* by Jan Brett. In this story, the sassy Gingerbread Baby is lonely and goes to the village looking for friends. He ends up getting chased out of the village and arrives home just in time to discover a batch of friends that Maddie has made for him! After the read-aloud, gather youngsters at the table and have them make friends for Maddie by making prints with the cookie cutters. Encourage them to drizzle a mixture of white paint and glue (frosting) over the prints and then sprinkle hole-punch dots (candy) over the mixture.

Note to the teacher: Use with "Listen and Do" on page 280.

TEC41070

TEC41070

TEC41070

TEC41070

Curious About Caves?

Make a Cave!
Beginning sound /k/

Focus on the /k/ sound of *c* with this easy-to-prepare activity!
Attach a length of bulletin board paper to a wall at student eye level.
Name one of the words below and have a child tell you if it begins
with /k/. If it does, have her add a stalactite or stalagmite to the
cave. Continue until each child has had a turn to add to the cave.

Suggested words: *corn, can, cap, cow, fin, camera, cake,
cup, cut, cab, rip, leaf, cot, coin, car, camel, cone, cart, bus,
call, card, cash, cat, cage, cork, cost, gate, count, copy*

Extend this activity with some
cave dwellers. The next day,
provide a bat stamp and ink pad.
Repeat the activity, focusing on the
/b/ sound and having students add
bat prints to the cave!

Cave Explorers
Investigating through pretend play

These realistic little caves are perfect for some pretend
play. Partially bury plastic flowerpots in your sand table.
Then add rocks to the table. (If desired, hot-glue Spanish
moss to the pots for an extrarealistic look!) Provide
people and animal figurines. (Plastic bat rings are a
fun addition to this center!) Youngsters engage in
pretend cave play with the props!

Live There or Visit?
Investigating living things

Some creatures live in a cave, and others come and go as they please. How do you tell the difference? Many creatures that live in a cave are white and may be blind or eyeless because they don't need the sense of sight when living in darkness. Make a copy of the cards on page 286 and color the bear, bat, pack rat, and cricket. Leave the other animals white. Then cut out the cards. Explain to youngsters the differences between cave dwellers and cave visitors. Then have students help you sort the cards according to whether the animals are permanent inhabitants or come and go.

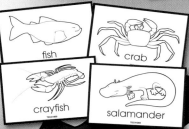

It's in the Bag!
Counting, making sets

Transform a paper grocery bag into a cave by rolling down the top of the bag and laying it on its side. Provide bat cutouts (or simply use several copies of the bat card on page 286) and a die. A child rolls the die and counts the dots. Then he counts out a matching number of bats and "flies" them into the cave. He continues until all the bats are in the cave.

Carole Beckman
Sea Gate Elementary
Naples, FL

Stalactites and Stalagmites
Expressing oneself through art, fine-motor skills

Youngsters get a fine-motor workout with this artwork! Provide tissue paper, patterned scrapbook paper, and construction paper. Demonstrate to youngsters how to tear paper to make long triangles. Then have students tear the paper and glue the resulting stalactites and stalagmites to a sheet of construction paper. What a fun and funky cave!

Picture Cards

Use with "Live There or Visit?" on page 285.

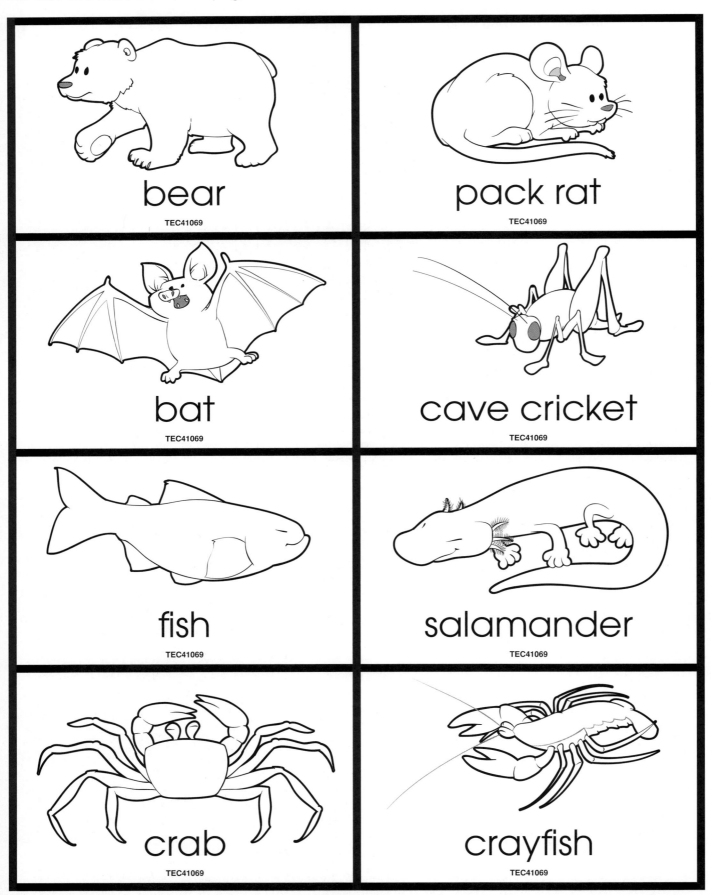

bear

TEC41069

pack rat

TEC41069

bat

TEC41069

cave cricket

TEC41069

fish

TEC41069

salamander

TEC41069

crab

TEC41069

crayfish

TEC41069

Teaching Trustworthiness

You can count on me!

A Lie or the Truth?

Help youngsters think about the terms *truth* and *lie* with this simple, lighthearted game. Place circles of yarn on the floor and label them as shown. Gather small blocks. To begin, ask students to explain what a lie is, helping them conclude that a lie is when someone doesn't tell the truth. Tell students a simple lie, such as "The sky is green." Ask students whether you told the truth or a lie. After students identify the statement as a lie, have a child place a block in the correct circle of yarn. Continue with other simple lies and truths. Finally, explain that these were silly lies to use for a game, but serious lies can be hurtful and can make people feel bad when they tell them. Encourage students to give examples of serious lies.

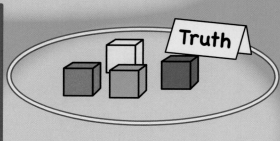

Truth

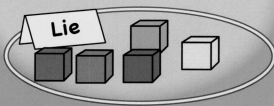

Lie

Do What's Right!

Ask students to share experiences they've had when someone lied to them and how that made them feel. Ask, "Was it difficult to trust that person again?" Emphasize that when people lie—even if it's just one lie—it's often very difficult to trust them. Sing this quick song to reinforce that honesty is the best policy!

(sung to the tune of "This Old Man")

Do what's right every day
When you work and when you play.
Tell the truth, be honest, never lie or cheat.
Do what's right—it can't be beat!

Suzanne Moore, Tucson, AZ

Follow Through!

Reinforce the importance of keeping promises with this no-prep activity! Get a puppet and gather youngsters. Ask your puppet, "What did you do yesterday?" Then have the puppet proceed to tell a story about promising her mom that she would pick up her toys. Have the puppet say, "It was really hard, but I got them all picked up!" Tell the puppet that it makes you happy when people keep their promises. It means that you can trust them. Have the puppet draw a smiley face on your board. Next, ask little ones to share times when they said they would do a good thing and then did it. Each time a child shares a story, draw a smiley face on the board.

Diane Friedline, Wee Kare Early Education Center, Clinton, MA

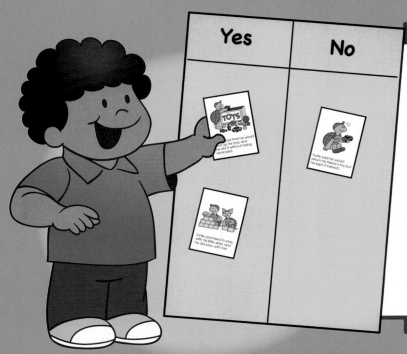

Trustworthy or Not?

Help little ones identify trustworthy behavior with this activity! Cut out a copy of the cards on page 289. Make a chart similar to the one shown. Then show youngsters one of the cards and read the words aloud. Ask, "Is Turtle being trustworthy?" After students discuss Turtle's behavior, have a youngster attach the card to the appropriate side of the chart.

Pass the Ball!

Here's a terrific story to help teach little ones about trustworthiness! Get a copy of *The Berenstain Bears and The Truth* by Stan and Jan Berenstain. In this story, Brother and Sister Bear knock over a lamp with a soccer ball. Then they lie to Mama and Papa about what happened. When the truth comes out, Mama tells her little cubs that it's important to tell the truth because "trust is not something you can put back together again." After the read-aloud, give a child a soccer ball and help him name what happened first in the story, using the illustrations as a guide if needed. Encourage him to roll the ball to a classmate. Continue in the same way with each subsequent story event.

Turtle said he would return his friend's toy, but he kept it instead.

TEC41070

Turtle promised to play with his little sister, and he did play with her.

TEC41070

Turtle said that he didn't eat a cookie before dinner, but he did.

TEC41070

Turtle said that he would pick up his toys, and he did it without being reminded.

TEC41070

Oozy, Squishy, Gloppy —Mud!

Meeting Mud Puddles

Participating in a song

Spotlight the squishiness of mud with this adorable action song!

(sung to the tune of "O Christmas Tree")

Oh my two feet, oh my two feet,	*Stomp in place.*
They like to meet mud puddles.	
Oh my two feet, oh my two feet,	
They like to meet mud puddles.	
It feels so good to squish around	*Do the twist.*
With all that mud upon the ground.	
Oh my two feet, oh my two feet,	*Stomp in place.*
They like to meet mud puddles.	

Cindy Hoying
Centerville, OH

Making Mud

Observing, predicting, comparing

Get potting soil, sand, and dirt. Then gather three children and give each child a clear disposable cup. Have each child touch the soil, sand, and dirt and describe them. Then encourage each student to spoon a different substance in her cup. Ask, "If we mix water with the soil, the sand, and the dirt, do you think all three of them will make mud?" Encourage youngsters to explain their thinking. Then have them mix water into the substances and discuss the results. Would they describe any of the results as mud?

Fingers and Toes

Exploring the sense of touch

Youngsters explore mud with their fingers *and* their toes at this center! Prepare a tub full of mud and place it at a center along with magnifying glasses and tools, such as craft sticks, forks, and slotted spoons. Encourage youngsters to explore the mud with their hands and the items. Then, after each child has had an opportunity to explore, add a tub of sudsy water and paper towels to the center. Have youngsters, in turn, explore the mud with their bare feet!

Melissa Anderson, James R. Wood Elementary, Somonauk, IL
Marcell Gibison, Early Children's Centers of Ephrata Church of the
Brethren, Ephrata, PA

For extra fun, place rubber worms in the mud! (Rubber worms are found in the fishing and tackle department of sporting goods stores.)

Making a Pie!

Tracking print, holding a book correctly

The next best thing to making a mud pie is putting together this booklet! In advance, mix flour with brown paint to give it a mudlike consistency and make a copy of pages 292 to 294 for each child. Have her color the pages. Encourage her to make brown fingerprints for dirt and mud on the cover and pages 1 to 4. (Make sure she adds lots of fingerprints to page 4 to indicate the mess!) Then have her make blue fingerprints for water on page 2 and for bubbles on page 5. Finally, cut out the pages and staple them together, in order, to make a booklet. Read the booklet aloud as she follows with her finger.

A Muddy Masterpiece

Developing fine-motor skills

To make this simple and satisfying process art, wrap a pink pipe cleaner around a marker and then remove it to make a pig's tail. Next, dip the tail in brown paint and then bounce, tap, and drag the tail on a sheet of paper. Repeat the process several times.

Recipe for a Mud Pie

by _____

©The Mailbox® • TEC41071 • Feb./Mar. 2014

One cup of dirt.

1

Add water.

2

Mix together until it's squishy.

3

What a mess!

4

Take a bath.

5

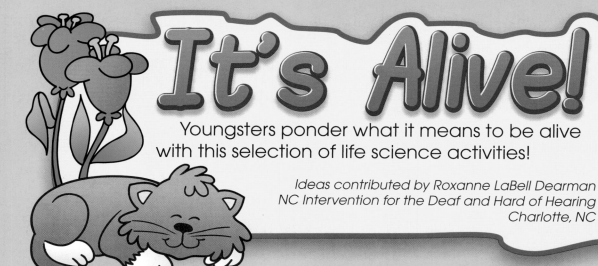

It's Alive!

Youngsters ponder what it means to be alive
with this selection of life science activities!

Ideas contributed by Roxanne LaBell Dearman
NC Intervention for the Deaf and Hard of Hearing
Charlotte, NC

Living or Nonliving?

Organizing data, developing fine-motor skills

Discuss with youngsters that living things need food and air and are sensitive to things around them, like heat and light. Label a sheet of chart paper, as shown, and provide a supply of magazines. Youngsters look through the magazines and cut out pictures of living things (such as people, trees, and dogs) and nonliving things (such as rocks, toys, and dishes). Then they glue them to the appropriate side of the chart paper.

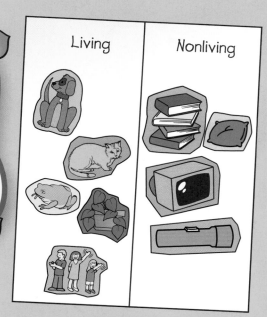

Let's Move!

Categorizing, developing vocabulary, developing gross-motor skills

In advance, write the plant and animal names shown on separate cards and place the cards in a basket. Explain that living things can move. But do we often see plants move? Discuss how plants cannot move like animals and people do. Plants can slowly turn toward light and they can grow, but they certainly don't fly or scamper up a tree. Have a child take a card from the basket. Read aloud the word on the card. If it is an animal, youngsters move about like the animal. If it is a plant, youngsters stand still. Continue with each remaining card.

Animals: *monkey, snake, penguin, fish, elephant, owl, crab, kangaroo*
Plants: *cactus, sunflower, pine tree, lettuce, tulip, celery, daffodil, oak tree*

How You've Grown!
Comparing length

Get a few baby shoes and gather a small group of students. Explain to youngsters that the shoes are similar to shoes they wore when they were little. Ask students to describe the shoes. No doubt, they will say how tiny the shoes are! Give each child a baby shoe and have her trace it on a sheet of paper. Then prompt her to remove her own shoe and trace it over the baby shoe tracing. Have little ones compare the tracings using words such as *larger, smaller, longer,* and *shorter.*

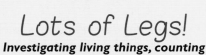

Different Habitats
Investigating living things, sorting

Cut out a copy of the cards on page 297 and add simple details to a sheet of blue paper and a sheet of green paper so they resemble an ocean and a rain forest. Place the papers on the floor and scatter the cards around them facedown. Have a child flip a card, decide where the animal lives, and then place it on the appropriate paper. Continue with each remaining card.

Lots of Legs!
Investigating living things, counting

Youngsters compare and count legs with this unique activity! Cut a supply of same-size pipe cleaner lengths (legs) and cut out a copy of the cards on page 297. Gather a small group of youngsters and set out a few of the cards. Invite a child to count the number of legs on one of the critters, count out the same number of pipe cleaner pieces, and then place them on the card. Continue with other cards and youngsters. Then ask children questions, such as "The jaguar has four legs. Are there other animals that have four legs as well?" Finally, have students count all the pipe cleaners that are on the cards to determine the total number of legs. Continue with other sets of cards.

A Learning Moment!

Youngsters may be quick to say that a sea star has five legs. Explain that those appendages are actually arms. A sea star doesn't have any legs; it moves by using tube feet on the underside of its body.

EARTH DAY!

Spotlight this important day with Earth-friendly ideas and activities!

The More We Can Recycle!

Participating in a song, learning responsible behavior

Lead youngsters in this engaging song to help them learn Earth-friendly behavior! Repeat the song, substituting *reduce* with *recycle*.

(sung to the tune of "The More We Get Together")

The more we can [reduce, reduce, reduce],
The more we can [reduce]
The happier we'll be.
'Cause my Earth is your Earth
And your Earth is my Earth.
The more we can [reduce], the happier we'll be!

Suzanne Moore, Tucson, AZ

The Importance of Trees

Making a set of ten

Make a supply of simple tree cutouts. Write "10" on a large sheet of blue construction paper. Also get a collection of number cards 5 through 10 and place them facedown. Gather two children and explain that trees are very important because they make oxygen, which we breathe. They also help make our air clean, and their roots keep the soil in place. Plus they make the earth beautiful! Next, say, "Let's make a forest with ten trees!" Have a child choose a card, name the number, and place the appropriate number of trees on the paper. Have the second child repeat the process. Then have the students count the trees together, noticing that there are more than ten. Help them arrange the trees so that only ten are on the paper and the remaining trees are nearby. Then prompt them to say, "We made one set of ten with [number] extras." Repeat the activity several times.

Reminder Buddy
Developing fine-motor skills

Have a child stuff shredded paper into a clean water bottle. Then help her glue fluffy craft feathers in the opening. Next, have her attach eye cutouts, a recycle symbol, and a tag labeled "Reuse and recycle!" (For extra fun, help her attach self-adhesive craft foam letters to the back of the bottle to show the message "Save a tree.") Encourage students to display their crafts in their homes to remind them to reuse and recycle.

Marilyn Horsley
Valley View United Methodist Preschool
Overland Park, KS

What Do You Love?
Responding to a book, dictating information

Make a class supply of green heart cutouts. Cut a large blue circle from construction paper and display it on your wall. Read aloud *I Love Our Earth* by Bill Martin Jr. and Michael Sampson. This nonfiction book shows colorful photos of green grasses, blue oceans, gray mountains, and brown deserts, encouraging love of Earth's various landscapes. Ask, "What do you love about Earth?" Write a child's words on a heart and then have him use a glue stick to attach it to the blue circle. Continue with each child until the cutout resembles Earth. Finally, have students stretch cotton balls and glue them to the cutout so they resemble clouds.

I love the lakes so I can swim.

Fishing for Cans?
Gross-motor skills

Here's an Earth-friendly take on a traditional fishing game! Cut out several copies of the cards on page 301 and attach a jumbo paper clip to each one. Then scatter them faceup on a sheet of blue construction paper (lake). Attach a magnet to a length of string and then attach the string to a yardstick or dowel to make a fishing pole. A youngster uses the fishing pole to remove all the items from the lake that shouldn't be there.

No Brushes Needed!
Expressing oneself through art

The earth provides all the tools needed for this project! Have students gather nature items, such as pinecones, leaves, twigs, and rocks. Place them at your art table along with shallow pans of paint in blue and green. A child chooses an item; dips it into paint; and then presses, taps, and brushes it onto a brown circle cutout. Continue until the circle is filled with prints and resembles the earth.

Hippos, Rhinos, and Leopards

WE'RE ON SAFARI!

Time to Travel!
Speaking, investigating living things

Kick off your safari unit with this discussion about travel options! Display a world map in your classroom. Then help youngsters find your location and attach a class picture to that spot on the map. Next, point out Africa and explain that this is where people go on safari. A safari is a trip taken to observe animals as well as camp and hike. Ask, "What types of animals do you think they have in Africa?" Have students share their thoughts. Then explain that people see a variety of animals while on safari, such as crocodiles, giraffes, rhinos, hippos, elephants, meerkats, zebras, leopards, and lions. Next, ask students how they could get to Africa, having little ones demonstrate the various forms of travel by pretending to fly, drive, and sail around the room.

Shelli Allen, Cane Child Development Center Wakefield, RI

Make a Map
Letter-sound association

Youngsters practice literacy skills with these super safari maps. Give each child a piece of kraft paper (or a section of a large paper bag) labeled with the following letters: *r*, *h*, *e*, *z*, and *l*. Next, help each child color and cut out a copy of the animals from pages 305 and 306. **For a less challenging version**, use fewer letters and corresponding cutouts. Next, have a child choose an animal and isolate the beginning sound of its name. Help her glue the animal on the appropriate letter. Continue with each remaining animal. Next, have her add details to the map, like trees, grass, and a trail.

Shelli Allen

For extra fun, have each child "age" the paper by crumpling it, smoothing it out, and then trimming pieces from the edge.

Let's Go!
Counting sets

Take youngsters on their very own safari! Attach different sets of animal cutouts around the room (see pages 305 and 306 for animal patterns). Then write the number of each set on a sheet of paper and make a class supply. Give each child a paper and a crayon. Have them tiptoe over to a set of animals with great dramatic flair. Then help them identify the animal and notice its characteristics. Finally, prompt them to count aloud to discover how many animals are in the group and then cross out the appropriate number on their papers. Continue for each remaining set of animals.

Lisa Shutters
Atkins Elementary
Atkins, IA

Totally Textured
Exploring the sense of touch

Print a photo of a Nile crocodile and a lion. (An Internet image search will turn up plenty of options.) Then place them at a table along with Bubble Wrap cushioning material, yellow or brown felt (or fake fur), and scissors. A child feels the cushioning material and felt and then cuts pieces of them as desired. Then she glues them to the appropriate cutouts to show the animal textures.

Mary Davis, Keokuk Christian Academy, Keokuk, IA

Happy Hippo!
Developing fine-motor skills

To make this simple craft, paint a paper plate gray. Next, glue eye cutouts and attach hole reinforcers (nostrils) to a simple hippo head cutout. Color a portion of two small gray semicircles (ears) with a pink crayon. Then glue the ears to the head. Attach the head to the paper plate. (If desired, glue a condiment cup between the head and body for extra dimension.) Then add gray semicircle feet and a yarn tail.

Angela L. Morlan
Holy Cross Lutheran Church Child Development Center
Colorado Springs, CO

 tip → These hippos look adorable displayed on a board and then covered with blue cellophane (water)!

On the Hunt
Taking part in an interactive read-aloud, recalling story events

Read aloud *We're Going on a Lion Hunt* by Margery Cuyler. This twist on the traditional bear-hunt story has a teacher taking her youngsters on a safari to find a lion. On the way, they pass a variety of animals found on the African plains. During the read-aloud, prompt students to act out the motions, such as slogging through the mud, climbing the trees, and swimming across the river.

Next, gather a few students and give each child a sheet of construction paper divided into six sections labeled as shown. Then have them recall the first obstacle the children in the story face (*mud*). Have students follow the directions below to illustrate mud in that section. Continue in the same way with each item. Encourage youngsters to use their papers to retell the story to their families.

1. **Mud:** Use a paintbrush to add a splotch of brown paint.
2. **Sticks:** Glue small twigs.
3. **Trees:** Glue a tree cutout (or draw a tree).
4. **River:** Drip blue-tinted water.
5. **Grass:** Glue thin yellow paper strips (or glue real grass).
6. **Cave:** Color the section black and then glue two yellow eye cutouts.

Four Little Zebras
Ordinal numbers, participating in a rhyme
This sweet little fingerplay is sure to be a popular part of your safari unit!

Four little zebras on the African plain,	*Hold up four fingers.*
Four little zebras see it's starting to rain.	*Wiggle fingers downward.*
The first little zebra went to stand beneath a tree.	*Hold up one finger; then place it beneath your cupped hand.*
The second little zebra said, "Hey, wait for me!"	*Repeat the action with two fingers.*
The third little zebra said, "I'm coming too!"	*Repeat the action with three fingers.*
The fourth little zebra cried, "Boo, hoo, hoo!"	*Hold up four fingers; then move fists to show crying.*
Then a passing hyena laughed, "Hee, hee, hee!	*Hold stomach while laughing.*
That rain won't hurt you, I guarantee!"	*Shake index finger.*

Diane Simmons, Coventry, RI

TEC41073

TEC41073

TEC41073

Animal Patterns

Use with "Make a Map" on page 302 and "Let's Go!" on page 303.

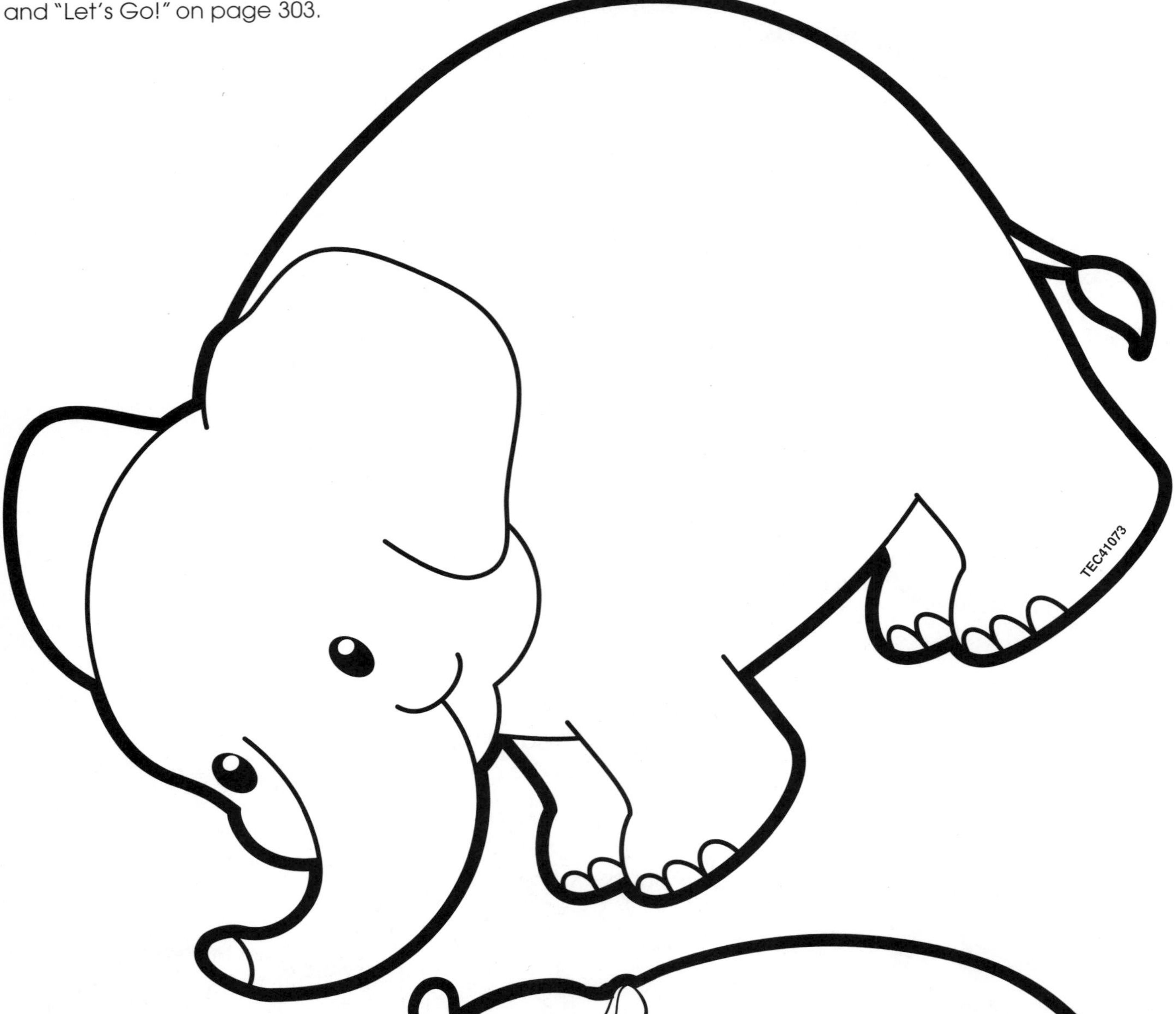
TEC41073

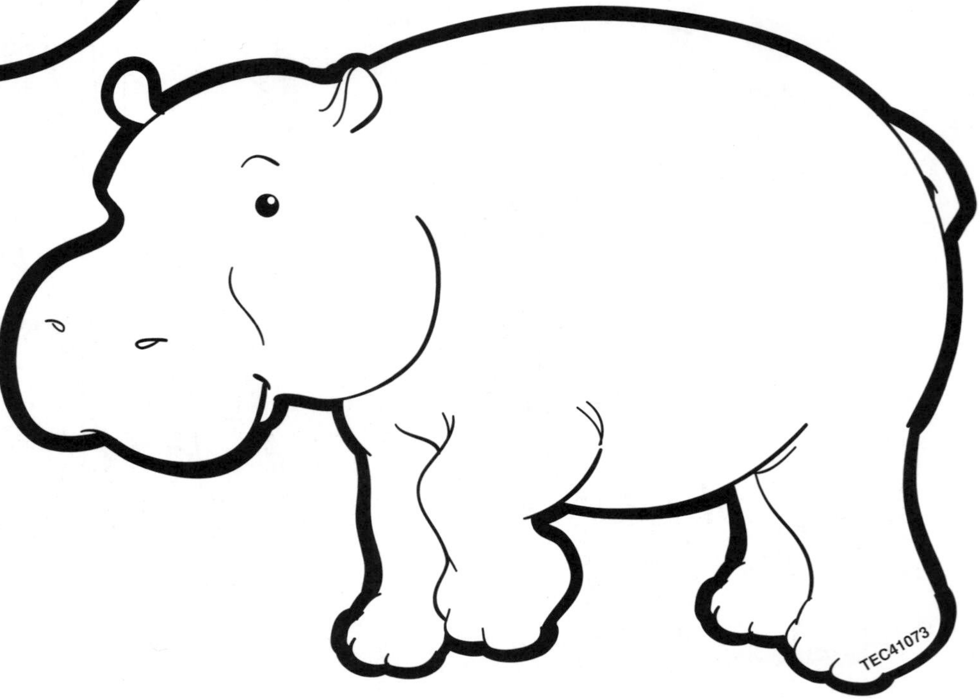
TEC41073

I Respect You!

Teach little ones the importance of respect for others with this selection of activities!

What Is It?

Respect can be a tough concept to understand when you're little! Help youngsters understand what respect means with this simple contract. Make a copy of a contract from page 309 for each child. Then gather youngsters and ask, "What does it mean to respect someone?" After several youngsters share their thoughts, explain that when you respect someone, you use kind words with them, you listen when they talk, and you believe that they are just as important as you are. During center time, meet with each child and show her a copy of the contract. Read the contract with her and then have her sign it to show that she will work at being a respectful person. Refer to the contracts throughout the year to reinforce respectful behavior.

April Pulfer, Grandview Heights, Columbus, OH

Friendship Bracelets

Encourage respectful interactions with these simple bracelets! To make the bracelets, laminate and cut out a head-shot photo of each child. Then hole-punch the photos and string each one on a separate pipe cleaner half. Twist the ends of each pipe cleaner together to make a bracelet. On random days, give each child a bracelet to wear. The child is encouraged to do one kind act or say one kind thing to that person during the day. At the end of the day, the bracelets are removed and placed in a basket for next time.

Carole Watkins, Timothy Ball Elementary, Crown Point, IN

How Do We Show It?

Spotlight simple ways to show respect with this chart! Write the headings shown on a simple three-column chart. Then ask, "How can you be respectful to your family?" Write down a child's suggestion on the chart. Then lead them in reciting the chant shown. Continue filling in each column with suggestions, reciting the chant after each one.

When I respect you
And you respect me,
We'll feel good inside.
That's a guarantee!

Family	Teacher	Friends
Say "please." Clean my room.	Give hugs. Raise my hand.	Share toys. Ask them to play.

Respectful Behavior Management

Youngsters learn respect from the adults around them. Show that you respect your little ones with a behavior-management system that empowers them! Place a chair in a quiet area of your classroom and label the chair "Power Chair." If a child is misbehaving, say, "[Child's name], you have a one." If the misbehavior continues, inform the child that she has a two. If she gets to the number three, tell the youngster to go and sit in the Power Chair to get her powers back. When a child feels that she has her powers back, she raises her hand and explains how she is going to act when she rejoins the group.

Marsha Phillips, #43 Lovejoy Discovery School, Buffalo, NY

The Preschool Pledge

To remind students daily to be respectful to others, begin the day with this pledge!

I am responsible for my actions.
I choose my words and thoughts.
By making smart choices,
I help myself and others.

Kimberly Duboise, Niangua Elementary, Niangua, MO

I Am Respectful!

_____ I will use kind words and actions.

_____ I will listen when people talk.

_____ I will say "please" and "thank you."

TEC41072

I Am Respectful!

_____ I will use kind words and actions.

_____ I will listen when people talk.

_____ I will say "please" and "thank you."

TEC41072

Let's Learn About
Simple Machines!

Youngsters explore simple machines
with these easy and engaging activities!

Fun With Inclined Planes
Developing spatial skills

Place lengths of cardboard (ramps) in different sizes in your block center along with a variety of toy cars and other wheeled toys. Little ones visit the center and lean the ramps against blocks. Then they "drive" the cars up and down the ramps. As students play, encourage them to notice how ramps help the cars move to lower and higher levels.

Cindy Hoying, Centerville, OH

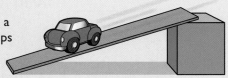

A Simple Song
Participating in a song

Lead students in singing this active song about three different simple machines: a pulley, a screw, and a wheel and axle. Before singing the song, show students a flagpole (pulley), a soda bottle (screw), and a toy car (wheel and axle). Explain how each simple machine works. Then have students sing this active song!

(sung to the tune of "Mary Had a Little Lamb")

A pulley moves things up and down,   *Stand up tall and then crouch.*
Up and down, up and down.   *Repeat the actions twice.*
A pulley moves things up and down.   *Stand up tall and then crouch.*
Now go fast—up and down!   *Repeat the actions quickly.*

A screw can help things open and close,   *Pretend to hold a bottle and open the cap.*
Open and close, open and close.   *Repeat the actions twice.*
A screw can help things open and close.   *Pretend to hold a bottle and open the cap.*
Now go fast—open and close!   *Repeat the actions quickly.*

A wheel and axle help things roll,   *Roll your arms over each other.*
Help things roll, help things roll.   *Repeat the action.*
A wheel and axle help things roll.   *Roll your arms over each other.*
Now go fast—roll, roll, roll!   *Repeat the action quickly.*

Krisha Salazar, Oak Tree Child Development Center, Fort Walton Beach, FL

Simple Machines Help!
Print and book awareness

Make a copy of pages 311 and 312 for each child. Then have each child follow the directions given to finish the booklet pages. Finally, help her cut out the pages and staple them in order behind a construction paper cover labeled "Simple Machines Help Us!"

Ada Goren, Lewisville, NC

Booklet pages 1 and 2: Color the pages. Glue a brown rectangle cutout (box) to the ramp. Add fingerprints (candy) to the jar.

An inclined plane helps Dog move the box.

1

A screw helps Bug take the cap off the jar.

2

Booklet pages 3 and 4: Color the pages. Draw something that Cat would like in the wagon. There are carrots in the crate. Write the letter *C* beneath the carrot.

A wheel and axle help Cat move his wagon.

3

A lever helps Rabbit open his crate of carrots.

4

INDEX

318